A GIFT OF LIGHT

ILLUSTRATIONS BY
RAGNA TISCHLER

CALLIGRAPHY AND DESIGN BY
TOM GODDARD

A GIFT OF LIGHT

A COLLECTION OF THOUGHTS FROM
FATHER ANDREW

SELECTED AND EDITED BY
HARRY C. GRIFFITH

INTRODUCTION BY
GERTRUDE BEHANNA

LONDON: A. R. MOWBRAY & CO LTD
NEW YORK: MOREHOUSE-BARLOW CO

© A. R. Mowbray & Co. Ltd., 28 Margaret Street, London
Library of Congress catalog card number: 67-31443
Originally printed in the United States of America
by Sowers Printing Company, Lebanon, Pennsylvania

Reprinted 1968, 1972 by offset in Great Britain by
Alden & Mowbray Ltd at the Alden Press, Oxford

ISBN 0 264 65573 7

CONTENTS

Introduction

To write an introduction to a book seems in part at least to presuppose that the introducer believes herself better known than the author, better equipped to entice a potential reader. In this case nothing could be further from the truth. Father Andrew is his own enticer, hand-picked by the Lord of Hosts, and my words are merely a public love letter in memory of the author—a letter not inappropriate since it was Fr. Andrew who first gave me an inkling of what Christ's love is. I had not heard of that modest English monk until some five years ago when I was sent a copy of one of his books. As I had respect for the spiritual maturity of the sender, I decided to skim the contents between appointments. That was a mistake, the mistake of treating a mighty banquet as if it were a drive-in snack. Although an Anglican celibate, Fr. Andrew knew more of what love is, human and divine, than all the ballads ever written, even than the New Testament itself, sifted, as it has to be, through the countless memories and viewpoints of its myriad translators. Almost as vital as knowing what love is, Fr. Andrew knew what it is not. In the relatively short period I'd been a Christian, I was still slipping up and down that ancient seesaw as to whether love was a state of being or a state of doing; was Christian love what I was or what I did? It was Fr. Andrew who answered the question. Prior to his death in 1946, he lived throughout the blitz in the heart of

London, and he tells how his first act each morning of
the war was to take down the blackout curtains. He did
it, he said, to let the light in, not the darkness out. I read
his simple words, then read them over and over. That
is it, I thought—that's it! That is where mankind gets
on the deadend track, trying to let darkness out instead
of allowing light in. The light is there for the accepting,
but no, we beat our chests, we cry *mea culpa, mea culpa,*
we pray and agonize and promise the little god we call
God, we drag behind us the rusty chains, the old tin-
cans of past, present and foreseen guilts, pridefully trying to earn that which is free. If someone said: "Every
morning I open the Venetian blinds to let the darkness
out," the little men in the white coats would come
running, yet that is precisely what we are saying when
we swear to do better, to be better, to dispel our human
darkness by means of our human light. Bless you, Fr.
Andrew, for making it clear that love is never what we
do; it is what we let be done to us. We are cups,
receptacles; our part is to hold ourselves right side up
that God may fill us with Himself. That is man's sole
destiny, and Fr. Andrew says it for the world to hear in
language an educated child could understand. To accept that destiny, to seek, to know and then to serve
the Lord of all creation, is our purpose just as it is the
purpose of the peachtree to bear peaches. To be born
to the proper parents, go to the proper schools, acquire
the proper academic degrees, marry the proper mate,
live in the proper neighborhood, belong to the proper
clubs, give birth to the proper children—is that all

there is? If it is, then I shall blow my head off, for
it is not enough. No matter what man knows or doesn't
know, there is more than that; just as the atom was
always awaiting our discovery, there are countless other
discoveries awaiting us. There is Love—the Love which
is the Light which alone can dispel man's darkness.
Fr. Andrew knew and knows that Love and tells of it:

> As I beheld Christ in silent majesty hanging upon
> His Cross, I saw in His gaze upon this world that
> there was no smallest trace of reproach, complaint,
> or blame, but only unutterable overwhelming love.
>
> I saw that His love was our judgment; and that that
> love was the greatest of all forces, the perfection of
> all power.
>
> Then there came to me three distinct messages.
> The first *to all the world*: His love went forth from
> Him in silent power but His silence said, with greater
> clearness than any spoken words, "Your sin has never
> lessened My love; here on the Cross I love you with
> an everlasting love."
>
> The second was *to all sufferers*: "I am God," He
> said, "Suffering is not natural to Me; as God I cannot
> suffer, but when I gave to certain of My creatures
> free wills and they admitted selfishness and sin into
> My universe, then of necessity there followed suffer-
> ing, and suffering can only leave My universe when
> sin has departed from it. But when I saw My crea-
> tures suffering, I took upon Me a human nature that
> I might make their suffering My suffering. All the
> suffering of the world is My suffering; I have made

it Mine in love; they that love Me may make My suffering theirs."

The Third was *to all the disillusioned, disappointed, bereaved, and out of heart:* "Behold Me," He said, "Here am I dying in the dark, and I came to bring light to the world. I am dying at the hands of hate, and I came to bring love to the world. Death is closing in upon Me, and I came to bring life to the world. But I remain true to My faith; dying in the dark I believe in the Light; killed by hate I trust Love; with death closing in upon Me I believe in Life; Do you then cling to your ideals; in any darkness still trust the Light, in any hatred still trust Love; and be sure that, though all consciousness be slipping from you and you yourself seem to be sinking into a void, eternal Life is yours."

So the message was given, and the silence was full of peace.[1]

Gertrude Behanna

---

[1] *The Life and Letters of Father Andrew*, p. 118, Morehouse-Barlow Co., New York.

Editor's Note

Henry Ernest Hardy was born in Kasauli, India, on January 7, 1869, one of the seven children of Colonel Edmund Armitage Hardy. He was educated at Keble College, Oxford, and received his theological training at Ely. He was ordained a priest of the English Church in 1895. He was one of the three founders of the Society of the Divine Compassion and later served as its Superior.

Better known as "Father Andrew," he was a man of great and varied gifts—poet, artist, thinker, and writer; and all his work in those various fields was dedicated to the one great purpose of his life, the glory of God and the service of His Church. Although he went as a missionary in Southern Rhodesia in 1932, he traveled comparatively little outside of England, and most of his 77 years were spent in Plaistow, London, ministering to the poor.

He died March 31, 1946, in Bushey Heath, Hertfordshire, England.

Father Andrew was a prolific writer, the author of nineteen books of prose, nine collections of poetry and six plays. The random extracts included in this book were taken from the volumes presently in print. The bibliography contains a complete reference, by page, to each quotation·contained in this anthology.

With extreme caution I have taken a few technical

liberties in the presentation of this collection of what I believe to be the finest of Father Andrew's thoughts. Some of the original verb forms have been changed to forms in current usage; and in rare instances, a deletion has been made of extraneous words and phrases. The insignificant changes are not shown in the manuscript; to have indicated them might have been distracting to the reader.

H. C. G.

Love

WE can write over the manger, "So God loved the world, that He gave His only begotten Son, that whosoever believeth on Him should not perish, but have everlasting life," and that ought to have been sufficient. But since it was not sufficient to write those letters in the whiteness of the innocency of Christ, they had to be written in the redness of the agony of His sacrifice, God using that precious blood that He took for love of us and that our sins caused to flow, to underline the declaration of His love for us.

The scene may appear common and the experience drab, but just as the stark hill of Calvary shines forever with the dawn above it, because of the Love that was revealed there, so our own ordinary life may have an extraordinary beauty, if by the loving oblation of our will it is really consecrated to the Lord of Calvary.

The highest love of all finds its fulfillment not in what it keeps but in what it gives.

"My God, My God, why hast Thou forsaken Me?"
—ST. MATTHEW 26:46

There are many things to which we cannot see the answer, but we can learn from our Lord to go without an answer. Let us bring our questioning to the Cross, and we can see in the light of His Passion the way of beauty leading onwards through the darkness, and we can trust that that way of beauty leads onwards and upwards to God.

When we think of the sorrows and afflictions which fall upon the innocent, and which in our poor limited light and judgment do not seem to have any value, we have to remember that there is such a thing as sin, and the consequence of sin must be an evil consequence.

The great God Who gave us these free wills of ours had to admit the possibility of evil brought about by the created will. A moral God, framing laws for the world, could not frame such laws as would make wickedness successful. What comes into the world through sin can only go out through suffering. If it paid, really and ultimately, to be wicked, then God would not be a moral God. Suffering had to come in for that reason. Again, since we are human, suffering has to come in as a warning. I must suffer in my body when it is burned or I should be continually burning my body. I must suffer in my soul when I do something wrong, or I might go on doing wrong. I can give that answer to the world's great "Why?" in its sorrow and suffering. But the best thing I can say to anyone who is sorrowful or suffering is still this: "I cannot give you an answer, but I can give you a reason for going without an answer." He had His "Why?" Did anyone ever cry out into the dark night that saddest of sad words with greater pathos and poignancy of pain than Jesus, Who has given the one answer to the riddle of life? He, hanging there, seemingly deserted by God, in the un-utterable darkness trusted God; and He, hanging there, looking down on the mocking faces of men, still loved men. They wagged their heads and said, "Thou that didst save others, save Thyself. Come down from the Cross, Thou Christ, and we will believe Thee." They jeered and jibed, and He made no reply. He seemed indeed the God-forsaken one, and what faith was His still to believe that the way of love was right, for, as Catherine of Siena said, "Nails had never held Him to the Cross if love had not held Him there."

He would not weaken a will by making things clear and easy for it; He would not bribe a will by some glittering promise of reward; He would not frighten a will by some threat; He would not break a will by force, or warp a will by something less than truth; He would win a will by the revelation of His love, love that was tested by hatred and stayed true, love that was tested by faithlessness and stayed faithful.

As long as we are going to get anything out of what we are doing, there comes in a certain measure of self-seeking. But when in complete darkness we choose love, when in the midst of happiness we choose what is right at the cost of happiness, we are somewhere near the Lord Who for love of us endured utter darkness.

A man may say that he does not believe in God, but if he says this he is confronted with the further problem of a universe that somehow or other came into being. The simplest explanation of a fact is as a rule the best. Should you go into the kitchen and find a kettle on the hearth, the simplest explanation and the best is that it is there because someone put it there, and you can follow up the thought with the further finding that it was put there by kind hands that wanted to make you a cup of tea.

We thank Him that, being what He is and knowing what we are, He still loves us and longs to have us with Him forever.

Our salvation, thank God! depends much more on His love of us than on our love of Him.

Gold is tested by being put in a crucible and letting the fire prove it to be gold. God willed that we should test Him on Calvary, and the fire of hate and sin wrapped round the Body of God as He hung there on the Cross, but nothing came forth from Him but love.

When a baby is born, the mother loves the baby because it is her own child, not because it is a good baby or because it loves her. God loves us because we are His children.

How beautiful always are the feet of those who take the Gospel of Christ to the souls for whom He died! There is a lovely story that comes from the mission-field. In Assam there was a mountain tribe of head-hunters known as the Lakher tribe. The son of one of the chiefs heard that Christianity had been brought to a neighboring tribe, and managed to send a request that this new religion might be preached to his own people. An adventurous missionary called Lorraine and his wife determined to answer this call, and went to live among the head-hunters. He did his best to express the love of God in nursing the sick and in any acts of kindness that were possible to him, and wherever he went he took a pencil and notebook and tried to learn the language. But it was quite impossible to become sufficiently proficient to write even one verse of the Gospel in the native language. Then a wonderful thing happened. A baby girl was born to the Lorraines, and the natives, who had never seen such a sight before, hailed the little white wonder as a princess and brought her gifts and paid her honor. The little one grew up with the native children and learned their language naturally, and as she grew older taught it to her father. So a little child led that hill-tribe of head-hunters to the knowledge of the love of Christ and the new life born of that knowledge.

Our salvation is the love of God for each one of us and our response to that love. Let us seek so to prepare our

souls that the Lord entering in may find a place prepared for Him.

It is not strange that, even when he was in prison and
chained to the soldier who kept him, Saint Paul was
able, while his mind held such thoughts, to write a
letter to faulty people filled with thankfulness.

It is not the will of God that because of bad drains
typhoid fever should become prevalent, but it is His
will that doctor or priest should love patient or parish-
ioner better than life, and so, if in going where love
calls him a man meets death, he need not think that it
was God's will that he should die, but he may be sure
that it was God's will that he should love, and can know
that death does not matter very much.

Humility arises from one's knowledge of the truth
about oneself, and charity from one's knowledge of the
truth about God.

I saw that His love was our judgment; that as the eye
must quail before the light of the sun because of the
exceeding brightness of that light, so the soul must
quail before His love because of the exceeding splendor
of that love; and that that love was the greatest of all
forces, the perfection of all power.

The wilderness really is the place where love is not.
There is no famine like that of the heart that hungers
for love and finds hate; or the mind that hungers for
truth and finds lies; or the soul that hungers for God
and feels itself in darkness. Our Lord knew all this to
a degree that we can never know. His sensitive heart
knew the very essence of hate in its contact with human beings: the field in the wilderness brought to His

mind and soul the supreme temptation to doubt and deny the love of God. But he fought through to love in the wilderness, as He fought through by love on Mount Calvary.

There He hangs, nailed to the Cross in the darkness, and He loves us still.

Saints whose souls are tuned to the divine harmony are specially conscious of the human discord, and it is always those who are most aware of the heavenly glory who are peculiarly conscious of the exceeding sinfulness of sin. As the soul realizes this truth, so the amazing condescension of God becomes more and more apparent. It would indeed have been a condescension on His part, if human nature had never fallen, to step down from the height of His own divine liberty and for the love of man to accept the limitations of human nature, so that He might teach man in his own human language of that home that He had prepared for him, and for which this life was to be a preparation. But after man had fallen, still to be ready to become incarnate and to be man's victim that He might be his Saviour is the revelation of a love beyond all human dreaming.

Our Lord loved to teach people by painting word pictures, and in the parable of the Good Samaritan He paints a picture of the love of God.

Humanity is as a man who has fallen among thieves and been robbed, and left there incapable of saving himself. We feel we have been foolish, that we have been robbed, that we cannot save ourselves. We have been robbed by our own stupidity. This man ought not to have been traveling alone.

The first person who comes along is the priest, who may stand for formal religion. Formal religion passes by and leaves humanity where it is. Then comes a type we know very well, the good-natured person who comes and looks at the man, and goes away and leaves him. Many people do that. They discuss the troubles of life and look at the slums, and go away and leave them.

Then the Samaritan passes by and comes where the man is. In that sentence is told all the deep mystery of our Lord's incarnation.

He came down to be in the poverty of the poor. He did not pass by. He did not come down and look at it and then go back to heaven. He did not come to tempted men and say, "You ought not to have that temptation," but He came to where the tempted man was. He came into the place of suffering, and willed that His own coronal should be a crown of thorns. The story of the Good Samaritan is the story of the Incarnation. It is a picture of the love of God.

Faith

WE have to remember that we shall never have *this* life again. We shall pass to other conditions, but in this life we have a unique opportunity of serving God and our neighbor in a particular way, and that will never come to us again. It is well for us to remember that we have our opportunity here and now to witness to God in this world and to do our part as well as we can while there is time. This life is the opportunity of faith. When we can see God, we shall be able to give Him our worship and our love, but we shall no longer be able to give Him our faith. That belongs to our period here.

One can but love and trust on, knowing that if our love, which is but a ray of the Divine Love, can be faithful, how much more will He go on beyond all our dreams of faithfulness.

As all those things that God has asked us to do, in forgiving one another, loving one another, all the directions He has given us, have proved His wisdom, we shall add to the wisdom we may have already found by trusting Him in the things we do not understand. Emmanuel Kant, who was one of the world's greatest thinkers, said, "When we know all things, we shall know that the Divine Wisdom was as wise in what He hid as in what He revealed."

I do not pretend to see light, but I do see gleams, and I know I am right to follow those gleams.

The writer remembers the beautiful words of an old woman who had had a great tragedy in her life, who came to him with her burden of pain and perplexity at the end of a mission service. He did his best to help

her with, of course, much pointing to the Cross of
Christ. The old saint bowed her head, and then looked
up with a light in her eyes and said softly, "I see, where
I cannot trace Him I must trust Him."

Faith is a spiritual virtue of the soul. It is not a natural
process of the reason. It is not, of course, contrary to
reason; and many who have possessed the finest reason,
the very finest minds that God has ever created, have
had the most sure and simple faith. It is not contrary
to reason, but transcends reason. It begins as an experiment; it becomes an experience. Science deals with
physical facts; faith with spiritual facts. Our outer life
relates to time and can be investigated by science; our
inner life is related to eternity and it is the spiritual
science of faith that must direct it.

It is only when we can say from the depths of our own
conviction and in the power of our own experience,
"Lord, I believe," that we make our first step into the
light of the everlasting dawn.

The first mark of the gift of faith is the love of truth.

The reward of faithfulness is greater faithfulness.

"Lord, I believe; help Thou mine unbelief," but let no
part of it stay in me. If my life brings me darkness,
help me to meet it with faith; if pain, with courage; if
bereavement, with hope; if joy, with gratitude; all
things with love and patience. So let my life indeed be
the expression of my faith.

Great faith is not the faith that walks always in the
light and knows no darkness, but the faith that perse-

veres in spite of God's seeming silences, and that faith will most certainly and surely get its true reward.

If the way of love were not the way of faith, it would not really be the way of love. If the way of beauty were not the way of faith, it would not really be the way of beauty. If you knew you were going to get something out of it, to that degree the loving way would not be loving, the beautiful thing would not be beautiful. As long as we know that we are going to get something out of being good, to get a return for what we give, there comes into what we are doing, however good it may be, something which is not pure faith. Let us take a parable. Suppose two men were cast into the ocean and neither could swim, and someone threw them a lifebelt which would only support one. One might say to the other, "You have the lifebelt, and I will sink." If he knew for certain that he had only to sink through a few fathoms of water and then he would be in a perfectly comfortable heaven, there would be nothing great about that sacrifice; in fact, it would not be a sacrifice at all. It is just because he does not know that there is nobility in his action. It is that wanting to get something, wanting to get peace, wanting to get heaven, that spoils our following of Christ.

The first converts to Christianity were not won by reading the Gospel or by the Gospel story in itself. There was one thing and one thing only that won the first converts to the acceptance of the Faith. They took knowledge of the apostles that they had been with Jesus. To meet an apostle was to have an experience, to have contact with a different sort of man, and the interpretation of that experience was the apostles' companionship with Jesus. They had been with Jesus and reflected His glory. It was this shining peace, this moral grandeur, this reckless faith, this uncalculating love, which made it possible to believe the impossible story that the crucified Carpenter was the Messiah, and that the Messiah was not just the Saviour of the Jews but the God Who created the whole world, working out His plan for the redemption of the world in the strange artistry of His love. Those who came within the circle of the influence of the apostles were able to make the experiment of faith which passed into the experience of realized fellowship with their Lord.

Coming back from South Africa, as the liner on which he was travelling home steamed through the Red Sea and was passing the Sinai range, the writer was joined by a fellow voyager. His companion stood silent for a while, and then with considerable passion delivered his soul of its permanent problem and continued craving. He cried, "I wish with my whole heart that I had your faith. I am not what the world would call an unhappy man. I am quite well off. I have got no skeleton in my cupboard. But I cannot see the use of life, and I can say with certainty that if this life were offered to me now and I could take it or leave it, I would most certainly leave it. I cannot see its purpose or its meaning or its worth. I only wish I had your faith and could make something of it." The reader may be sure that an ejaculatory prayer went up to God for guidance to help this poor pilgrim on his way, and the contact was certainly blest to both, for many were the talks together before the ship deposited the voyagers at Tilbury Docks on their return to England. It all depends upon a man's view of life. If it is looked upon just as a pleasurable occasion that is the theory by which the life is lived, it does not work. This man was travelling for pleasure.

He had a wife and family, and they were all fond of one another, but they had no sense either of the permanence of life or its holiness, and really the first perception depends on the second, for there is no reason why life should be permanent if it is not precious and holy. The conversation that actually followed this first declaration comes back to the memory. The end of life is not happiness but holiness.

Life is for the creation of character, and character is formed by the greatness of choice. As choice is made by faith that it is worth making a sacrifice that the best may be, so the character is enriched by that choice and shaped for the vision of the holiness of God which will be granted to the purified soul. But the first step must be the step of faith. This man craved for the holiness of God, and nothing that the world could give had brought him satisfaction. Only when he could say, "Hallowed be Thy Name," would there come to his soul the peace for which he longed.

Sacrifice

SURELY nothing of more importance than the conversion of Saint Paul has happened in the history of the Church since Pentecost. His was one of the greatest minds God ever created. No doubt the first questioning came to him when he heard the speech of Stephen, a man who had the history of their race at his fingers' ends and could show how it all led up to the coming of Christ as the true Messiah. How often, when a man is beginning to be convinced, does he fight against the conviction when it will mean a very great change in his own life! So Saul of Tarsus went to Damascus to fling himself against what seemed to him to be the menace of a new heresy.

On the Damascus road God revealed Himself, and in a blinding flash there came to Saul the beginning of the conviction that Christ was indeed the fulfillment of all that Moses and the prophets had been leading up to. If Christ was the living, everlasting God, there must be a complete revolution in every part of his life. For three days, in darkness, without food or drink, Saul fought in a terrible spiritual conflict the challenge that had come to him. He had gone forth to destroy something which he firmly believed to be wrong, having behind him the authority of all the important people in his religion, and he had now to come to the conclusion that that authority was wrong, and that the very thing he had set out to destroy was the true Gospel of God. He was too big a man to shirk the issue. He came to his conclusion and took the consequences. He became the slave of Christ.

If we really believe that the Man Who was nailed to the Cross of Calvary is our God, and hung there for love of us, we cannot wish that our following of Him should not be a very costing thing.

People often say, "My mother was such a good woman: why should she have suffered?" or "My boy was such a fine boy: why should he have died?" It is a very natural thing to say, but when we find ourselves saying it we should look at Jesus crowned with thorns, holiest of all, loveliest of all, and yet suffering more than all. His whole life, as He lived it amongst the people of His time, was a beauty and a glory, a flame of love passing by, and yet He was crucified.

It is our behavior in life, not so much what we do as how we do it, not so much what we suffer as how we take it, that marks us as the disciples of the Divine Master.

Life is a great vocation, and Christ's disciples will put into it all they can of sacrifice, love, and labour. The Christian character is the flower of which sacrifice is the seed.

All of us have our parts to play in building up the New Jerusalem. He, Who came down from the mountain of prayer, had to ascend the mount of sacrifice. The apostles had to realize that, if it was a wondrous thing to see Him transfigured on Mount Tabor, it was an even more wondrous thing to see Him disfigured on Calvary.

All people are prone to accept the current idea of authority and kingship prevalent in their day. Any book which portrays with sufficient accuracy the manners and behavior of ordinary people in any age, gives us a picture of a multitude following, as sheep follow the bell-wether, the common ideas of the time. Thus, we have the mystery of fashions, when all over the world people suddenly cut their hair off or grow their hair long or yield to some fashionable practice, even though it may cause them great discomfort. The trend may be more or less harmless, or it may cause them great discomfort. Men who are in advance of their time have stemmed or tried to stem such drifting, and we see the herosim of the artist, the poet, the prophet who refuse to follow the multitude, and make their lonely sacrifices to truth. But what a weary travail such a sacrifice often entails, and is there anything harder to bear than complete misunderstanding? To bear it is the price that martyrs pay. As writes Elizabeth Rundle Charles: "To know how to say what others only know how to think is what makes men poets or sages; and to dare to say what others only dare to think makes men martyrs or reformers or both."

The end of devotion is attained when the complete taking of all things meets with the complete giving of all things. Death, the great taker, is defeated when he meets Christ, the great giver. The supreme devotion of our Lord's life was consummated as He laid down His life for His sheep and yielded His spirit in perfect faith to His Father. The true end of devotion is the gift of ourselves and all we have to God.

The multitude sought to make Christ a king. That is the supreme mistake. He *is* King. We have to let Him make us His subjects. If we try to make Him a king, we shall be fashioning a crown and a throne of our own conceiving, and clothing Him with our ideas of royalty. The people who sought to insult Him were all unwittingly right when they said of Him, "He saved others: Himself He cannot save." That was absolutely true, and that was His true royalty. If He had saved Himself, He could not have saved others with a true salvation. Every good soldier, every good doctor, every true friend follows in His steps. If a soldier saves himself, the battle is lost. If a doctor saves himself, the patient may die. If the friend saves himself, he is false to his friendship.

There is a French proverb, "It is the first step that costs." It is only partly true. That which is much more true is that the real costliness of life is in being true to one's faith when it has led to a way of sacrifice; being true to one's word when it means an unexpected cost; being true to one's cause when it is in peril; being true to one's friend when he is perhaps discredited, in dire straits and in danger.

If we bring the loaves and fishes to Christ, and are content that they should be broken as well as blessed, they become means of union, uniting us with God and one another. If we can but surrender ourselves, our possessions, our talents, our business, our trade, wholly to God, then He can bless the gift, however little it may be, and make it food for the many.

If suffering went out of life, courage, tenderness, pity, faith, patience, and love in its divinity would go out of life too. Terrible as suffering is, nonetheless, it is the condition of some of life's very greatest beauties, even as the wounding of the shell is the condition of the pearl's appearing.

Humility

WE have to recognize quite clearly that sin is sin, but we may learn many things through our falls. A person who is to hold high authority and whose duty may be to pronounce judgment on others should be endowed with very real humility. We can understand how the fact that he had denied our Lord helped Peter, the prince of penitents, to maintain lowliness of heart. The first lesson a sinner may learn from sin is the grace of humility. Our Lord said to Peter: "I have prayed for thee, that thy faith fail not: and when thou are converted, strengthen thy brethren" (Luke 22:32). The gracious words teach us two other lessons that may be learned from sin: dependence upon God and sympathy with sinners. The sinner who comes to the Friend of sinners can find not only forgiveness, but humility, dependence upon God in faith, and sympathy with other sinners and the power to help them.

We cannot know God, if we do not understand the revelation of Christ. Why do we worship Him? Because He would come down and be cradled in straw that no little slum child might ever feel his God wanted a better cradle than he. That is our God, and that is what Christmas means, that the great God shrank down to the dimensions of a child to reach children, that He took quivering, suffering human flesh that He might be beaten and wounded and reveal His heart to humanity.

There is no enemy to prayer like pride, and spiritual pride is the death of spiritual prayer. God's mercy will always humble us while He leads us, for the ascent of the soul to the highest is conditioned by the descent of the self to the lowest. Our Lord's spiritual ascension was manifest in earthly action as He washed the feet of sinful men and died at the hands of sinners on a cross in the dark night of Calvary.

When there was murmuring and discontent among the apostles, what happened? Jesus called them to Himself. He brought them into His own atmosphere. He taught them the true values of life. He said to them, "Among the Gentiles people seek places of importance. That is the way of the world. But you are not going to be like that. The greatest amongst you is he that is serving most." When we can completely forget ourselves and think only how we can best serve other people, we pass from the evil atmosphere of selfishness to the peace and creative power of sacrifice.

The Incarnation reveals to us that generosity in giving which is part of the adorable character of God. Coming to His world and making Himself known to it, He willed to come in the most generous way possible, in the way which would be the greatest help and blessing to those who most needed help and blessing. He came to lay His head in the place of poverty. He willed that His cradle should be the poorest of all cradles and His quilt the cheapest of all quilts, and He lay there in the generosity of His self-oblation with the wood of the manger beneath Him and the straw of the stable about Him, the great God manifest under the guise of the poorest little Baby that ever was born.

All through His life He was consistent. He saved for Himself no privileges. He did not go off to heaven for weekends! He, Who made all things, made chairs and tables, and yokes for oxen, and oars for boats, and the simple things the village needed; in the utter generosity of His love sharing truly and really, without the slightest bit of unreality in it, the actual life of a working man of that age and generation.

In His death His generosity reached its climax. There we see Him not passing from the Mount of Transfiguration through an adoring company of angels to that glory which was His by essential right, but making His death for us the way of life, and bringing comfort and comradeship to two wrecked lives as He hung on the mount of shame betwixt the thieves; and as He passed from His Passion to paradise, it was a thief whom He took for His companion as He made His human entry into the world of spirits.

Prayer

PRAYER, which begins with asking, thinking, and thanking, becomes at last the spiritual outgoing of the whole personality of God in union with the love and patience and Passion of our Lord Jesus Christ, in act and thought, silences and sufferings, more than in uttered words.

The habit of living in prayer is no easy matter, and our prayer experience has, and must have, its cycles and seasons. Winters of patient waiting and apparent deadness are succeeded by springs of hope and quiet mellow summers and autumn glories, to be followed by more winters and new springs, as the soul passes through its seasons of spiritual experience as a branch of the living Vine. The voice of God called us out of nothing into being, and that same voice calls us on to the deliberate life of worship; and the utterance of our own life is to find union with the utterance of this living Voice which is ever leading us on to a more understanding obedience and a purer condition of contrite love.

Often I have heard people say that they could pray to God while they were walking about and doing their chores, but that as soon as they knelt down they were plagued with distracting thoughts. The truth about that is that they prayed best when they were least conscious of themselves.

Intercessory prayer, prayer "in the Name of Jesus," is this. It is not suggesting to God ways of helping: it is not reminding God of things. It is our faith that God is helping: it is our remembrance that God is remembering. It is putting ourselves at the disposal of God that He may use our will power, heart power, psychic power, as waves of spiritual love and energy given to Him and made free for Him to use in blessing those whom we are allowed to cooperate with Him in helping, and whom He can only help humanly if we put our humanity at His disposal.

Jesus our Master, do Thou meet us while we walk in the way and long to reach the heavenly country; that following Thy light we may keep the way of righteousness and never wander away into the horrible darkness of this world's night, whilst Thou Who art the Way and the Truth and the Life art shining within us. Amen.

"The kingdom of heaven," said our Lord, "is within you." The best prayer is not that which feels most, but that which gives most.

The first thing that we have to determine when we come to prayer is that we will really come to God with our wills and our minds and not just our mouths and our knees.

Migratory birds fly very high, for three reasons. First, at a high altitude they can see better where they are going. Secondly, they are above the predatory birds that might prey on them. Thirdly, in that rarefied atmosphere they can fly very swiftly and easily. That is a parable of the way of prayer. Our souls are migratory souls. Our home is not here, but with God, to Whom we must seek to rise on the wings of prayer. We want to get high to see where we are going. What are we striving for? Not for any end of our own, but that we may cooperate with God's will in God's world. We must strive to rise above the noises and the fuss and all the complications that distract us and rob our lives of their own spiritual quality. Again, in the rarefied atmosphere of the presence of God we shall attain to that simplicity of intention which will enable us to pass swiftly to our true goal, the communion of our souls with God.

Father, no human eyes have seen Thee at any time, but Thy blessed Son hath revealed Thee, and in the mirror of the light that shines from Him we see Thy glory. Father, I am seeking. Help me to find.

We want to come to our prayer in the spirit of a disciple. Always saying the same prayers just as a matter of duty will be to lack the spirit of discipleship of prayer. The disciple will always have something to bring to the Master. There is the day's work behind him, for which he wants criticism, correction, forgiveness, and teaching; there is the day's work before him, for which he wants guidance and direction. Therefore in his prayer there will be much listening and expectant silence, and obedient readiness for alteration or abandonment, as the holiest way of the Master may be communicated to his listening spirit. It makes the whole difference if, instead of bringing a plan to Him and asking Him to bless it, we come to Him as disciples to learn what *His* best plan may be, quite ready to abandon our own plan and to have all our ideas altered as we kneel before Him. Perhaps we were going to ask Him *how* we should do or say something: we find it would be much better not to do or say anything at all. When the Master has finished giving us His advice, as in simple prayer and meditation we lay our souls before Him, we shall not get up immediately and go away, but in meditation we shall contemplate the

Master's own work, His skill in doing the thing we have bungled. Then we shall cease from looking even at the Master's work and contemplate the Master Himself. Himself—myself—my work—His work—Himself. That will be the kind of order in which we bring ourselves and our interests to Him.

"I saw the river which must be passed in order to reach the kingdom of heaven, and the name of that river was 'Suffering.' And I saw the boat which takes so many souls across the river, and the name of that boat was 'Love.' " So wrote a certain Soeur Eugenie. And to the good sister no doubt was granted the vision of a light shining upon the waters, and the name of that light was prayer.

If we discover that our attention has wandered when we have been saying some prayer, do not let us repeat the prayer but just renew the attention. A wandering mind cannot always be helped. What is critical is that there should not be a wandering will.

The great answer to prayer is the power to pray more. We have not so much to think whether prayers are answered as whether prayer answers. In a certain sense our Lord's prayer was not answered, but how His prayer answered! The cup was not taken from Him, but with what magnificent courage He drank the cup.

The cross is the revelation of the wonderful power of suffering love offered for other people. When perfect Love was robbed of every weapon except the power to suffer, Love took suffering and found that to be the most powerful weapon of all. The greater the love the greater the power to suffer and the greater the suffering;

but Love never lost faith in the power of love. If prayer is, first of all, faith in God, it is, secondly, the offering of oneself in love for other people; and this double energy is revealed in the rays that break through the darkness that shrouds the Cross.

There is an old legend that the sun shone down on Calvary, and the shadow of the Lord's Cross moved round as the sun moved round, till the sun shown full upon the face of Christ and the shadow of His Cross touched the cross of Dismas. From the shadow Dismas saw that face, and there passed that mystery of love from the Christ on His Cross to the creature on his cross. Dismas understands and takes up the great prayer. "Thy kingdom come!" says Dismas: "Lord, remember me when Thou comest into Thy kingdom," and the royal answer comes back, "My will shall be done. To-day shalt thou be with Me in Paradise." We see the great prayer being prayed and having its dynamic spiritual power. "Thy kingdom come. Thy will be done."

Lord, I am out of heart with myself. I have fallen to a sordid level of selfishness. I should have made a sacrifice of my own pleasure, and I did not make it.

I have been an unjust steward. I knew quite well that I owed Thee an hundred talents, and I took my bill and erased the whole amount. I did not even make it fifty. I know my own unfaithfulness must affect the faithfulness of others and make them less faithful.

Lord, I am very sorry. Thou, Who knowest all things, knowest that I love Thee. Help me really to repent, and save me from being interested in my own penitence. Keep my thoughts on Thee, and let me hold Thy hand and get up again and go on. Lord, forgive me.

Peace of God

OUR Lord said, "To him that hath shall be given, and from him that hath not shall be taken away even that which he seemeth to have." He was teaching us one of the laws of the mind. If we disbelieve in the kingdom of God within, and doubt our power to conquer in the strength of Christ within us, we make ourselves weak; that "have not" in our consciousness actually prevents our "having" in our experience. If we will only believe truly and triumphantly that the kingdom of God is within us, we shall begin to find that it is coming about all around us. There is in people's minds an idea that if they could only have a certain environment, and possession of wealth and power, the result would be peace and a kingdom of order. But our Lord taught us an opposite method of approach. He showed us the other way round. We cannot enjoy circumstances of peace if we have not peace within us; we cannot enjoy riches if we have not the true riches within us; we cannot enjoy freedom if our spirit is not free.

In Eastertide we may consider the Resurrection appearances of our Lord, and how they bring us solutions of life's problems.

His first appearance is to a watcher by a tomb. Mary Magdalene is not only a type of the artistic temperament, the lover of beauty, but, as she kneels by the sepulchre, she is the type of the mourner, out of whose life all that was worth living for has gone. When she knew for the first time what it was to be loved with a pure love, the whole of her life was changed, and she saw a glory in life that she had never seen before. But when she had seen that love die in the dark, as she sobbed by that garden tomb it must have seemed that the whole of life was a complete betrayal, that the best one could say about it was that it was a garden with a tomb in it, into which sooner or later every fair thing would go.

Surely faith and hope were left behind that day, when love knelt by the tomb of Christ in the garden; or did she remember those words spoken by another tomb, "Said I not unto thee, that, if thou wouldst believe, thou shouldst behold the glory of God?" We do not know, but this we know, that to her, the mourner, came the risen Christ, with the revelation of the continuance of personality after death, the justice of God that should overrule the injustice of earth, the glory of God manifested in the love which was stronger than death. We know that in the midst of life we are in death; Christ has revealed that in the midst of death we may be in life.

If we really believe that God is always with us, how it will transfigure our lives! How it will transfigure the journey in the bus, the work in the office, if all the while we are thinking, "Here am I, having contact with God. Inasmuch as I do kindness to these people, I am ministering to Him: inasmuch as I receive kindness from them, I am receiving it from Him. This mixing up with my fellow human beings is a sacred thing. This office is Nazareth, this street is a street of Galilee." There stands One among us Whom so often we do not know. Then somebody's face shines, we see a soul through the eyes and a Presence through the soul. All our life, in our home, in our work, in our street, becomes a tremendously exciting thing, because God is always there, just such a little veil between us and Him.

To make a little parable: if tomorrow I wake tired, have a difficult duty to do and a difficult person to meet, and I let my imagination dwell on these three difficulties,

I shall probably not get up, shirk the duty and avoid the person and be defeated. But if, as soon as I wake, I stay my imagination on my Lord rising a great while before day, on the heroism of the martyrs and the quiet power of the saints, then I shall rise with power in my will and peace in my mind and go forth to meet my day.

> "There came a woman having an alabaster box of ointment of spikenard very precious; and she brake the box, and poured it on His head."
>   —ST. MARK 14:3

Sometimes an act, which may not seem very important to someone who does not know the meaning of it, may mean a tremendous amount to the person who does it. To this poor woman the breaking of the alabaster cruse and the pouring of the rich ointment on our Saviour's head symbolized the giving of the whole treasure of her womanhood, the wonder of her life.

Our life is meant to be poured out, to be spent. All the great lives we have ever known have been poured out for others. When our Lord said those strange words about the harlots and publicans going into the kingdom of heaven before the Pharisees, His meaning appears to be that it is better to spend badly than not to spend at all. He seems to say: "You Pharisees have hoarded your lives, so that no one has been the richer for them. These people have squandered their lives, their sins are many, but nevertheless they have spent them." It may even be that it is better to spend money badly than to be a miser, to spend talent unwisely rather than not spend it at all. We can, and it is a very sad thing, spend our treasure badly, but we can learn by that spending.

Here is this woman, who has spent the treasure of her womanhood badly. Now she comes to Jesus, and in the light of His purity she sees the darkness and squalor of her life. But she pours out her treasure on His head, and in that act finds peace, and not only did she get blessing for herself but the whole house was filled with the odor of her spending. So the whole Church is enriched by every sacrificed and consecrated life.

It is a great and peaceful joy to wend one's way on a summer evening through a beautiful countryside to some quiet resting-place, enjoying the songs of birds, and the evening light, and the radiance of the setting sun, or to listen to music that steals into one's consciousness and reveals thoughts too deep for words, or to know the wonderful silent sympathy of a friend in the contemplation of some perfect work of art. But all these very real and lovely experiences fall altogether short of, and are not to be compared with, the unutterable content of the soul that, becoming aware of the reality of the Presence of God and His infinite love, is able to say, "Hallowed be Thy Name."

We may be in the most sinful surroundings and have purity in ourselves, or in the most depressing surroundings and have hope in ourselves. In all places and at all times Jesus is near us, and to such as are ready to receive Him His word is ever: "It is I; be not afraid."

There are three chief thieves that rob us: idleness, ignorance, and impurity. Idleness robs people of effort and development; unemployed people are being robbed of their true self-expression as men. Ignorance is a thief; people are always being robbed through ignorance of riches that ought to be theirs. Again, impurity is a thief; it persuades people that a sensation which lasts for a moment is the true riches, and all the while impurity is robbing them of their peace and their communion with God.

To the man who has fallen among these thieves comes the Good Samaritan. To the man who has fallen among the thieves of idleness He brings work, and shows that life is a vocation. To the man who is ignorant, who does not know what life is for, Jesus comes as the Light of the World, and tells him that he is a son of God. To the man whose eyes are blinded by impurity the good Lord comes with eye-salve, that he may be saved from lust as he learns to see the vision of the true Love.

"If you have seen anyone die, consider that you must pass by that selfsame road," says Thomas à Kempis in the *Imitation*. Death is inevitable for all of us, but we know that enfolded in the shadows of the valley is the presence of Christ. We are not alone, and our passing is not a passing out but a passing on. Each one of us is born into this world through a mother's pain. As in the acutest moment of her travail is enfolded the

birth of a new life, so in the travail of our dying is enfolded our birth into the world beyond. The life of the
child is unfolded here: our life in God is unfolded there.
What is enfolded in pain may be unfolded in glory.
The last unfolding of all will be love.

Any man who is trying to make his life indeed a worship of God and a service of man, may think of whatever suffering and shadows and discipline this brings
him as the marks of the Lord Jesus. If we seek for
liberty, we shall never find it. If we yield ourselves
wholly to the service of Christ, His service is perfect
freedom. In the life beyond the veil the spiritual body
will bear the marks of the Lord Jesus, each soul free,
yet each soul marked, and all souls having fellowship
in Him.

Once returning from his Saturday night ministry, the
writer was surprised to find a policeman waiting for him.
He had brought a message to say that a man, dying in
one of the great London hospitals, was asking for his
ministry. He recognized the name as belonging to a
man who had once held the rank of a major in the
Army, and after that had lived in many lands and been
guilty of many rogueries. He had twice served sentences
in Dartmoor and had an intimate inside knowledge of
many prisons. But, like many another, his was a com-
plex character, in which amongst the evil there shone
the light of the true Faith which he had been taught.
The man had fallen down in the street. He probably
had had a heart attack, and he was very far gone. He
lay in a little cell-like ward in the casualty annex of
the hospital. He had a tube in his nose and was being
given oxygen, but he knew his visitor at once and was
able to whisper, "God bless you! God bless you!" The

minister whose privilege it was to give Communion to
that dying man can never forget how his face was
transfigured when he received the immortal gift. He
passed to God in utter peace very shortly after. Through
all storms, through all buffetings of the waves of life,
his soul's barque floated into the calm waters of the
haven of God's love. So he came home to port. Christ
had turned the bitter water of his life into the wine of
his acceptance and another poor thief went home with
Him to Paradise.

Penitence
and the Soul

PENITENCE is the resurrection of character. If we are satisfied with our own condition, we shall certainly not try to rise to something higher. Where there is no penitence there can be no progress. The under side of the splendor of the saint's robes is the sackcloth of his penitence.

Get back to the Cross of Jesus again and again and again. When you are in a temper get down on your knees and do not get up until the temper is gone; if you doubt the love of God get down on your knees and look at the cross and let the presence of Jesus have power over you until the doubt of God's love has gone; if you are going to do something wrong get down on your knees and look at the cross and think of God's pain and do not rise from your knees until your will is right and you can make the sacrifice that God demands.

When Mary and Joseph lost the Holy Child, they had to go back to where they had lost Him, and we have to do that over and over again in life.

If our bodies and our minds need their right nourishment, how much more do our souls, which are our real selves. There is indeed something lacking in an education which, developing the body and the mind, neglects the culture of the soul. A great deal of the trouble of the present time is due to this, that while we have accumulated the means of production, men have lost any clear and definite notion of the end for which they are producing. You may satisfy your body with indulgences, and your mind for a while with distractions, but your soul must have its rest and its goal and its true food, or you yourself may be starved in the midst of plenty. "Adversity is hard upon a man,"

wrote Thomas Carlyle, "but for one man who can stand prosperity there are a hundred who will stand adversity." This is true, because while prosperity caters for the indulgence of the body and the diversion of the mind, adversity calls out the nobility of the soul.

Thackeray used to say that the story of Cinderella was the loveliest tale that ever was told. All such stories of one who has sat in ashes and then wedded the king's son, like the beggar-maid who found favor with King Cophetua, or Esther with Ahasuerus, are types and parables of the Christian soul entering into her true royalty. All have their significance in the deep truth that underlies our life, that God made us for Himself, and His possession of our being is at once our glory and our peace.

There cannot be at the same time acceptance of sin and acceptance of God, and so the soul, despairing or defiant, goes on its way in the darkness of its own distress.

If the eye sees wrongly, if it is injured or blind, then the world is either seen with a distorted vision or not seen at all. In the same way, if the conscience, the spiritual faculty of the soul, is distorted or asleep or altogether undeveloped, a man is like someone walking in the dark in a strange place.

The real burning of the candle at both ends is exercising body and mind without exercising the soul. Times of spiritual refreshment, however we come by them, are much more important than times of physical rest.

Philosophy

U NLESS moral and spiritual development goes before intellectual and mechanical, the march forward will be downwards and not upwards.

Our acts are really always, whether they are good or ill, the expression of ourselves. When we change, they change. But whatever they may be, they have the value for good or ill which we give them.

In the spring lies the hope of the harvest. It is the same with everything that we do. It is the first intention that matters. It is not the victory that is so important as the fight. It is not the achievement so much as the labor. As we look back upon our lives and try to find the first note of reality in them, the first bud of our spiritual spring will be that movement, whatever it was and however it came into being, when in pure joy or real sorrow or with a spirit of true quest we ourselves sought God for Himself. It is in the spring of things, in the purity of the first intention, in the sincerity of the first desire, that the whole of our life's reality lies.

Do not fight temptation: ignore it. Except to some trusty friend (and then never for sympathy but only for strength), never speak about your temptations to any one, and do not speak about them to yourself. Dwelling on them and talking to yourself or other people about them is the worst thing you can do. The positive affirmation of the opposite virtue and the ignoring of the temptation will be your best weapons.

We can never really suppress desires, and we are not meant to. If there is a stream flowing through some part of the country, and the people who dwell there wish that it would not flow past their doors, it is no use for them to try to dam up the stream: the result would be a flood that would break all barriers. What they must do is to dig another channel for it. Suppression of desire is not the right remedy. The redirection and consecration of desire is the right remedy. The wrecking caused by perverted desires has caused Puritans and people of that type to try to suppress desires, and again and again an age of Puritanism has been succeeded by an age of licentiousness, where the flood which has been gathering behind the barrier finally broke that barrier.

If we just like a person, all we want is that person's happiness. People who are superficially patriotic want their nation's prosperity. But a father who really loves his son would sooner see him dead than dishonored. Because he loves his son, he wants something much more than just that that son should be happy. He wants him to be splendid. We surely must want for our nation something much more than prosperity. We want its integrity, its real liberty from fear or the desire for gain.

The highest privilege there is is the privilege of being allowed to share another's pain. You talk about your pleasures to your acquaintances; you talk about your troubles to your friends. It is only to the person you know and trust most that you can tell your greatest sorrows.

The outlook depends upon the person who looks out.

What is a flower? It is just the dust of the earth that God has touched with life, and so brought about this threefold miracle, a loveliness of form and fragrance and color.

Beauty abides. All sin and ugliness are but transitory. They are contrary to the mind of God, and so have no abiding quality. That which is God's will shall surely come about at last. God has all eternity in which to do His great work and to bring into being the loveliness which is according to His heart. But we can see the track of His presence. The mysterious beauties of the world are surely the prints of His passing. The sunset over the tranquil sea, the deep green shadow under the overhanging rock, the sea-gulls wheeling on unmoving wings, all witness to a beauty beyond and above man's mind. And all these fair things abide. They are going on now. Let us try to turn our minds from all the material ugliness to the material beauty which is surely meant to be, and to remember that the cause of beauty abides always. Our world is scarred and made hideous, but how quickly nature clothes it with green again. The outward appearance may be destroyed, but the hidden inward cause abides ever. Let us take all the toll we can of material beauty. Let skies, dawns, and sunsets, the flowers in our gardens, and every lovely thing we see, lend their treasure to our experience.

There is such a thing as clock-time, and there is spiritual value, which is above time and belongs to eternity. Life is to be estimated not according to its clock-time length, but according to its eternal value. One rich moment is better than many languid years.

It is the indwelling reality that makes everything real. Music which is simply noise is not really music. It is the indwelling theme, the indwelling soul, which makes the music real. Just the painting of pictures is not art, the stringing of rhyme is not poetry, the going to services and so on is not religion. In all things it is the indwelling, unfolding, ever-rising beauty, as in the world of nature the oak is drawn out of the acorn, the glory of the flower is drawn up from the seed through the earth, by the power of the sun's rays. The loveliness of the naked trees in the winter, of trees in their summer or autumn clothing, is all drawn out from the hidden mystery where beauty is born. So we draw near to Him Who loves us that He may indwell us, because the indwelling mystery is something that cannot be filched from any soul that draws near in faith.

The writer remembers many years ago, before he was ordained, being with the father of the present Archbishop of Canterbury at a festival at Ely, when he was a student at the theological college there. Another bishop came into the room and commiserated Dr. Temple on the state of his eyes, for the old man was blind or nearly so at the time. "Aren't your eyes a great trouble to you?" inquired the bishop. "No," was the almost fierce reply. "Why should they be? They are not my fault." A thing that was not his fault was not going to trouble him. The lesson of that experience has never been forgotten, and the writer has ever prayed that he might learn to worry over his sins and to think lightly of his misfortunes.

It is much easier to do than to be: it is much easier to make professions than silently to achieve reality.

I had a particle of flint in my shoe. I took my shoe off and cast out the flint. The flint had set up an irritation and I was tempted to scratch it, but I knew that was foolish. The cause of the irritation had been removed; the irritation would pass, and it did. When we bring our troubles to God it is like casting out the flint; when we scruple about them it is like scratching the sore.

There are people who are afraid of the superficiality of life, and there are those who are afraid of its seriousness. If we look into ourselves, we shall find that we are constantly doing what Adam did in the story of the Garden of Eden, and hiding behind the trees lest we should see God. We hide behind life lest we should see the Author of life. We hide behind effects because we will not face their causes. We let events blind us to their meanings.

If we are confronted with a beautiful picture or are allowed to hear noble music or come to the knowledge of some heroic act, our reaction to these things is really a blessing or a judgment. If we see nothing in them, we take nothing from their beauty, but they are our judgment. The light has come to us: we have preferred darkness, and the light condemns us.

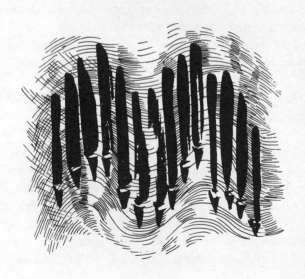

Nature of God

THE judgment of God is not the judgment of one who wants to find out where we are wrong in order to condemn us, but the judgment of one who knows we are wrong and wants to help us.

Our Lord not only wants to forgive us, but to save us from the conditions which made it necessary for us to ask for forgiveness. He wants not only to forgive us our sins, but to give us the power to conquer our sins. As we learn that sin is not just breaking a law, but that it is hurting a heart, we begin to see what a cruel thing sin is. When we find that the Heart we have hurt still loves us, and yield to the communication of that love, something more than forgiveness comes to us: there comes to us the power to conquer sin. What has been called "the expulsive power of a new affection" alters everything, and we enter into a new freedom.

Never judge God by suffering, but judge suffering by the Cross.

For a long time now, we are told, darkness had covered the earth. Then within the darkness Jesus spoke, "My God, My God, why hast Thou forsaken Me?" This is the first verse of the Messianic Psalm (Psa. 22), which our Lord had pondered again and again, and which He knew to be fulfilled in Himself. He had no tinsel dreams of a Messiah Who would rule by force. Our Lord, Whose Spirit had inspired the prophet to see the Servant of God as a man acquainted with grief, knew that the Messiah must be a suffering Messiah, as He could only save suffering man through suffering. So when He said these words, there was no falling from the perfect confidence in the Father. There is not the cry of one who doubted, but of One Who shared life's darkest problems, Who experienced to the death life's direct pains. Nevertheless, He felt to the full the agony and distress of the deepest spiritual temptation.

The Incarnation and the Cross are the way in which God has come to us through the storm. When He came to the Apostles, He did not bid the storm cease and then come to them over calm water; He did not bid Peter come on calm water. But He came through the storm and over the storm, and bid Peter do the same. He came to Mary Magdalene the harlot from the long fight with the devil in the wilderness. He came to Dismas the thief through the storm of Calvary. He, a tempted man, came to tempted men; He, a storm-tossed voyager, came to storm-tossed voyagers. God does come to us through contrary winds, God does come to us walking over the stormy waters of life.

"What have we to expect? Anything. What have we to hope for? Everything. What have we to fear? Nothing." These words of Dr. Pusey are suitable for the occasion of the times we live in. We do well to make up our minds to *anything*. We in our generation ought not to desire that, having entered into the labors of those who have gone before us, we should escape from any travail pangs that may bring to birth the better things that we should be hoping for, for those who follow us. Dr. Pusey looked out on a Church in which the sense of the supernatural seemed extinct and spiritual experience practically unknown. Altars were receptacles for hats and umbrellas, and at St. Paul's Cathedral there were on Easter Day only six communicants, and yet he hoped for "everything." We have been allowed to see many things that he hoped for restored. But we have to look beyond the Church, not

only to hope for a Church at unity in itself and one
with the rest of Christendom, but for a world won for
Christ, in which men have forgotten how to make war.
The only thing we have to *fear* is our own instability.
We have nothing to fear for God's cause. Truth will
prevail, the kingdom will come, God's will be done, if
not by us then by others.

Man's crude idea of God is that He is a sort of mil-
lionaire in worlds, with the power to fling about miracles, Who would do just what He liked, when He
liked, and how He liked, without any thought of
economy or care for detail. But if we look at our Lord's
ways of acting, we find two characteristics about them,
continuity and care. He takes what is and lifts it up to
something higher, and He never wastes anything.
When He was confronted by a hungry multitude He
did not say, "I am God, and I will send down manna
to them. I will make palm-trees spring up in the wilderness and give them a splendid banquet." He said to the
apostles, "If you will give what you have wholly to Me,
we can feed this multitude." He took what they had,
and blessed and brake it, and the multitude was fed.

In seven words our Lord sums up His mission: "I am
the Light of the World." In His sacred heart was the
ineffable longing that those to whom He came should
come out of the unrealities of their twilight to the
reality of His light, and being set free from their sins
they might enter into the light and glory of the knowledge of God. As He came that we might have life more
abundantly, so He came that we might have light more
abundantly, and the light eternal is one with the life
eternal. It is the knowledge of the Father Whom He
came to reveal.

This is the kingdom over which the Messiah presides, but it is the Messianic kingdom in the same sense as He is the Messiah, and we shall only learn to understand it as we understand Him. Just as He was misunderstood, so the kingdom has been misunderstood. Saint Peter believed in the Messiah, but he found it very hard to believe in a suffering Christ. He had to learn the character of the King, and what a long, long time it has taken us to learn something about the character of the kingdom! It is the representation in this world of the kingship of Christ, a kingship of wounds, not weapons; of love, not force; of peace, not strife.

All doors open from within, and it is the dweller in the house who has the key. If any one wants to come in, he must knock. There is the door of the vision of God, and we must wait His will to open that door for us. God lives behind the door of His own mystery. He says to us, "Knock at My door" (Luke 11:9), and that is all we can do. We can but knock; we must wait for Him to open. The revelation of God can only come from God.

It is very interesting sometimes to share religious experiences. The writer was told of one such by a friend. Her first consciousness of God as a Being came when, as a tiny child, she was allowed to visit the studio of an old man who modeled artificial flowers in wax. The studio was a converted loft with big windows at the top of a rickety dark staircase. When the door was opened, the incomer was momentarily dazzled by the bright light. It was a riot of color. Flowers were everywhere. The venerable artist worked at an old table near the window. The child would stand entranced and watch him, with his white hair and shaggy eye-

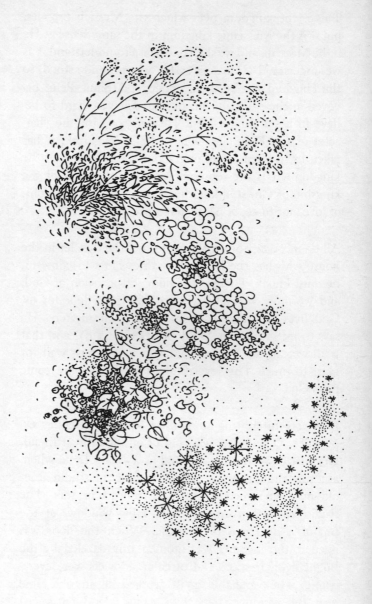

brows, a watchmaker's eyeglass screwed into one eye, as he molded the tiniest parts of a flower with the real flower pulled to pieces as a pattern. One day she stood enraptured by a little bowl of the daintiest flowers imaginable. The old man came and stood beside her. He was tall but he stooped, and his eyes were very blue. "Do you like them?" he asked. "They are wonderful," she breathed: "I cannot believe that they are not growing." "Nay, child," he said, as he laid his hand upon the little head, "I can make beautiful flowers, sometimes almost perfect flowers, but only God can give the spark of life." She never quite forgot his words, and they have stayed with her ever since. "Only God can give the spark of life" to a nation, a group, or an individual soul. What may seem perfect, seen superficially, unless God is working in it has no real life or growth.

When Saint Peter was brought out of prison, the iron gate opened of its own accord. That he could not open. But when he came to the house of Mary, the mother of John Mark, the door there did not open. He had to knock. Again, the chains fell from Peter, but he was told to put on his sandals: they did not put themselves on. God does not do for us what we can do for ourselves.

God has been working His purposes out in all the great movements of history. Greek thought, Roman order, and the Jewish genius for religion were the immediate preparation for the Gospel; and by the same token all that is best in modern movements and all that is true in modern science will, we may be sure, be gathered into the treasury of the Church for the ultimate purpose of the glory of God.

It was not just in spite of His distresses and difficulties that the Divine Master learned obedience and offered the perfect Sacrifice for us all, but *through* them. Hate brought Him thorns and He turned them into the Crown of Life, and the worst day in His life's experience, the Friday that brought Him murder and a death in the dark, He changed into the best day in His love's expression, so that we call it Good Friday.

The Life and the Resurrection of our Lord taken together are the witness to the reality of the presence of God behind life, to His character and to His deity. If our Lord had risen from the dead and there had not been during His earthly existence the perfection of His life of love, the Resurrection would simply have been a marvel which set people wondering, and would really have been incredible. On the other hand, if our Lord Jesus Christ had not risen from the dead, we should have wondered how the great power of God Who is behind life had failed to give some sort of witness that this Life, which was so perfect, was indeed a life of union with His will and expressive of His thought.

As the Archbishop of York, in a talk one Sunday, pointed out, there is nothing essentially divine in a marvel. To quote the Archbishop: "In the Life which it crowned and the Death which it cancelled, the Resurrection has set its seal on our faith in the divinity of Christ." His Life and His Death witnessed to the love which makes Him divine: His Resurrection witnessed to the divinity expressed through that love.

Again, the Resurrection appearances of our Lord bear a charactertistic stamp of humility and holiness and utter disregard of any kind of desire to "score" off those who had injured Him. He did not appear to Caiaphas or Pilate and say, "Here am I Whom you condemned. Who is master now?" He appeared to the humble and the penitent, to doubting Thomas, to heart-broken Peter, to the harlot whom He had reclaimed. To these poor friends the Lord of Life appeared. The Resurrection is a witness to the Character and the Divinity and the Mind of God.

Our Lord came to reveal the God Whom eye hath not seen, and in the mirror of our Lord's life and revelation we can, though under a veil, look upon the face of our King.

She who first saw the King's face looked upon a little Child, and those who are led to found nurseries and work at children's hospitals and child welfare have seen the face of God in a little child.

The boys and girls of Nazareth, the men who carried boats to the shore, the men who came to Him that He might fashion the yoke for their oxen, saw the face of God in a Carpenter at His work. He is the Lord of Labor, and the common work of every day may be the divine employ of God Himself. Those who seek to bring help and comradeship and beauty into the life of the factory and the shop and the street have seen the face of God in the Carpenter of Nazareth.

Since God mingled His life with our life, and knew our temptations, and in loneliness sought the way of holiness, so every one who strives to keep a pure ideal and bring purity and chivalry and truth into life has seen the face of God in the tempted Christ.

Again, since He suffered torture of mind and soul and body, those who see human suffering and long to succour it, who themselves accept suffering and seek to sanctify it, whose sympathy compels them to go amongst the suffering, have seen the face of God crowned with thorns.

Lastly, those who have felt the compelling call of God to come apart, who have felt there is nothing so worthwhile as prayer, have seen the face of Christ in prayer on the Mount of Transfiguration.

Some people might look at a picture and think it good or bad, and their opinion might not matter because they did not know much about art. The thing that would matter would be the opinion of an artist. A man's next-door neighbor might think him a good or bad man, and that opinion might not matter. The opinion that really does matter is the opinion of our Lord Jesus Christ. He is the great artist of life, and the value of an act is the spiritual quality which He sees in it. He sat at the door of the Temple and saw people giving their alms, and He was not in the least impressed with the clattering offerings that fell from the hands of the rich, but He was moved to speak immortal words about one poor woman who gave a farthing.

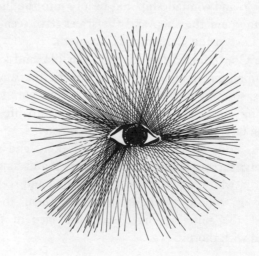

Nature of
Christian Life

FAITH in God will be shown by claiming the whole of life, science, labor, art, sex, everything, as God's kingdom. The Church must claim the world, for the kingdom of God will only come when the Church and the world are one.

Our belief in the living Christ is something much more than just belief in His survival after death. There is nothing necessarily divine in that. Our Lord's death is the consummation of His perfect obedience to the divine law of love, which is the eternal will of His heavenly Father. What from the earthly side of things looked like death and failure, from the heavenly side of things was manifest as the perfect victory of love. His death was the revelation of Eternal Love, which His resurrection revealed to be Eternal Life.

The Psalms are the spiritual music of the Church, the songs of souls rising to the heart of God, music that is sometimes ineffably joyous, sometimes unspeakably sad, but always beautiful as it throws back to God the echoes of the revelations which have come from Him "at sundry times and in divers manners" to the apprehension of His children.

> "I determined not to know anything among you, save Jesus Christ, and Him crucified."—I COR. 2:2

That is one of Saint Paul's final decisions. He had a very harassed and troubled life, and no doubt he was a man of quick temper, which he was often tempted to lose. But after thinking all sorts of things about people, he comes to this conclusion: "What I am going to think about everybody is just this, that here is someone for whom Jesus Christ died. I don't want to know

anything more about him than that." Another final
conclusion of his we read in Galatians 6:14: "God
forbid that I should glory, save in the Cross of our
Lord Jesus Christ, by Whom the world is crucified
unto me, and I unto the world"—"I am going to think
of every trouble as something that brings into my life
the Cross of our Lord Jesus Christ, and I am not going
to think anything about it save that it gives me some
share in bearing His Cross."

Those are two great conclusions to come to. Whatever people are, Christ died for them. It is not our
business to judge them. All people with whom we come
in contact bring to us this recommendation, that they
are the brethren for whom Christ died. Whatever
trouble comes to us, that trouble is our share in the
Cross of our Lord Jesus Christ, and as we learn to glory
in the Cross so we can find joy in our share of it. It is
our part in our Redeemer's travail in bringing a new
world to birth.

The Old Testament is God's picture-book, and we get
all kinds of things shown to us there in pictorial form.
We can think about them and meditate upon them,
and learn many secrets from them. In that picture-
book of God we have many stories of servants of God
receiving communications from Him and of their re-
actions to those communications. Sometimes, like
Gideon's father and mother or Samson's parents, they
did not realize till afterwards that it was a communication from God at all. Afterwards they thought,
"Something has come to us from beyond, something
not of this world." Things sometimes come to us that
we did not think of for ourselves, thoughts and understanding, and we see things clearly that we did not see
before. Our lives are not haphazard things.

The Christian Church is a body of pilgrims coming home to the heart of God.

"The kingdom of heaven is like unto treasure hid in a field." What a lot of things the kingdom of heaven is like—a grain of mustard seed, a net cast into the sea, leaven in a loaf, treasure in a field—all very simple and close at hand.

The way of pain is the way of sympathy. I should find it very hard indeed to pray to a God if I thought that I could suffer something which He had never suffered. I should find it very hard to worship a God if I felt that I could plumb a deeper depth of suffering than He could know. But I know I cannot. Whatever I may suffer, I can never suffer a tenth of what He suffered. And I know very well that I can only understand the temptations of tempted men because I myself am tempted. I can only have true sympathy with suffering people if I myself can feel pain. So this inexplicable mystery of suffering may be to us the way of sincerity, may give us the chance of proving to others that we are true, of proving to ourselves and God that we are worthy of the name of the children of God. It may also be the way of sympathy, linking us all together.

The Bible is really the guided, inspired word of man about the Word of God, but there is only one real Word of God, and that is our Lord Jesus Christ. The Bible gives us the inspired prophecy that looks forward to His coming, and the inspired memoirs of men who wrote about Him when He came, but the one Word of God that abideth forever is our Lord Jesus Christ. He is the everlasting Word that shall never fail, He is the everlasting Revelation that shall never pass away, the everlasting Life in Whom alone we shall find our perfect peace.

Religion is not proficiency in the fine art of mystical knowledge, but just the love of God and our neighbor.

There is little good in filling churches with people who go out just exactly the same as they come in: the call of the Church is not to fill churches but to fill heaven.

The only real victories are spiritual victories. The only real defeats are spiritual defeats. However much things may appear to be won or lost on the material or physical plane, it is the spiritual sphere behind the outward appearances that is the sphere of reality. Prophets and saints have always known this.

We are not made to rest in this world. It is not our true native land.

Worship is the making of the whole life one act of responsive love to the creative glory of God.

One of the most cogent arguments for the truth of our Lord's Resurrection is the effect it produced in the apostles. These men, who had all fled away at the Crucifixion, gathered courage such as they had never had when they had His actual living presence with them, courage which enabled them to meet martyrdom, and power to preach the Gospel of Christ and convince others. It is inconceivable that these poor frightened men could have gained this courage and power for any reason but the reason they themselves alleged, that they had contact with their living Lord.

But they gained something more, an understanding of our Lord's character and nature, which we see growing and growing in their letters, the Epistles. The men who had expected that He would bring down fire on the Samaritans who did not give Him a welcome, whose idea of the Kingdom was a kingdom in which they would sit on His right hand and His left, were learning more and more the mind of Christ. Our Lord never worked a miracle for display or as an argument for His divinity, and after His Resurrection He did not appear in all His glory to those who had condemned Him and tread them under His feet. The apostles learned the mind of their Master in His Resurrection as in His life, that it was not just by rising from the dead that His divinity was proved, but by His life of love and holiness. They realized that by that very way in which He revealed Himself they were to reveal Him, by the way of love rather than by miracles, and they went forth determined to serve Him in the way of sacrifice, lowliness, and service.

David was not only a poet, he was also a prophet, and gave the message of the prophets. The message of the prophets in the Bible is that we can trust God's integrity, and that we have to meet His integrity with our own. We have to be the sort of people who, if we say we will do a thing, will do it, whatever it costs us. The message of the Psalms is that the true worship of God is the spiritual worship of the heart, which is to be revealed in the life.

In the sphere of earth we lose all we love: in the sphere of heaven we find all we lose.

Natural heredity means the transmission of qualities from parent to offspring; but there is a supernatural heredity which is the fruit of baptismal grace, as to the

Christian is transmitted something of the holy heredity that comes from God our Father to us His children through Christ our Saviour.

If people give up their religion because someone forgets them or slights them, it is shown that their real treasure is in being thought of and considered, and not in Jesus only.

There are three ways of regarding the relationship of the Church and the world.

Some people look upon religion as something altogether apart from the world, and the Church as a place of escape from the world. That is one way of looking at it. You enter into the Church and save your own soul, and do not care at all about the world.

Another way of looking at the world is as a battleground, in which character is made. There is no real relation between the Church and the world, but we have to endure things in the world for the formation of our characters.

The third and right thought is that the function of the Church is to restore God's order in this world. The world is meant to be the revelation of the will of God, and sin came and destroyed the order. Then our Lord came, and ordained and founded the Church, which is His Body, to restore God's order in the world. The function of the Church is to bring about a right fulfillment of the will of God. In the Incarnation we see the Body of Christ in the world, showing forth healing and comfort to the world, and offered for the world in perfect sacrifice. The Church of God is meant to be in the world, shedding forth light and love and healing to the world, and offering its continual prayer and sacrifice for the world.

We cannot make a better resolution than to learn more deeply the secrets of faith, hope, and love, and make those secrets the foundation on which we build the fabric of our lives.

Faith that behind life there is something better than a force, something kinder than a fate, the Presence of a Father. Faith that He loves each one of us with a not less individual love than that which was revealed to us in the stories of the lost sheep and the lost silver and the lost son. Faith that the kind, sad eyes that looked down from the Cross were the very eyes of God Himself. Faith that can believe that when we sin we are not just breaking His rules but breaking His heart. This faith will give life to our prayer and reality to our penitence.

Because our God is, as St. Paul said, "The God of Hope" we shall join hope to faith, and both to love. We could not have a hopeless faith any more than we could have a faithless love. If hope will go to school at Calvary, hope may learn to become a fellow-scholar with Dismas the thief, and to see the kingdom coming even though the King be crowned with thorns.

While we learn some of the secrets of faith and hope, we shall learn also to know that when the light of faith dims down and that of hope seems to be extinguished, the light of true love need never lose the least portion of its radiance, but may shine on in the darkness, and gain perhaps a truer radiance from that darkness. Faith will teach us prayer, hope will teach us service, love will teach us consecration and worship and bring to faith its beauty and to hope its wings.

God added to His divine knowledge a human knowledge, a human experience. He himself came down to this earth, and went into the wilderness and sought the will of an unseen Father. He himself hung in the darkness on a cross, with that thought perhaps in His soul, "Thou God seest me, dying here in the dark for man," and He commended His spirit in that dark night to the seeing God Whom nevertheless He could trust through it all. Let us take to ourselves this thought of the God Whom we trust seeing us, knowing us. Let us try to make it the purification of our lives, knowing that He knows all that we do. Let it be an inspiration that He sees all that we do and that the humblest task may be an offering to Him. Let it be a great comfort to us to know that He understands all our failures and if we are doing our best, we may leave the rest to Him.

A French writer said, "Our Lord was no more taken in by the piety of the good than by the vice of the wicked." Our Lord knew just what was superficial and what was real in people. He could see that there was a great deal of piety that was just on the surface, in the outward expression, and did not go very deep. He could also see that there was a lot of vice which was very much on the surface and not the expression of the real person.

It is possible under a thousand forms to be seeking oneself. The recognition of this is not something to put us into an agony of scrupulosity. It is a warning, which we may spice with a sense of humor. St. Francis de Sales said, "We shall be fortunate if self-love dies half an hour before we do." Self-love crops up again and again and again. We are imperfect people, and we have to be very patient with ourselves, realizing that in everything we do there is a great deal of self, but not allowing that to make us downcast or unhappy, rather letting it help us to see that we have to go on working at our own development more and more that everything in our lives may be the true expression of a real love of God and our neighbor. If it were, of course, we should be saints, and we are not saints yet.

The thought of the harvest sets a very living parable before our minds. We shall not have a harvest if we do not sow anything in our fields. If we do not sow love, we shall not reap love: if we do not sow thoughts, we shall not reap ideas: if we do not sow faith, we shall not reap heaven.

Then the harvest brings us the thought of faith. The farmer has a heap of seed, and what is he going to do with it? He is going to fling it away! The text, "Cast thy bread upon the waters," is meant quite literally. People went out in boats and flung seed upon the waters of the Nile, and, as the water subsided, the seed sowed itself in the muddy ground. A good old priest once said, "A great many men cast their bread upon the waters, but they tie a string to it first!" That is where we fail. We will not take a risk. Most of us need much more real faith in our religion.

Again, there is the thought of patience. The farmer has to wait a long time, and perhaps see his harvest destroyed. It is going on with patience that makes our character.

Then the day comes when the harvest is reaped. We do not want to limit the mercy of God, but our Lord does say that you cannot go on serving God and Mammon. There must come a harvest; either of all your little failings, your little unstable ways, ultimately producing the harvest of a person who is not worth much; or of all the little hidden acts of perseverance and faith and sacrifice, which will result in the harvest of a character which has a likeness to the character of Christ.

The apostles had their differences; Saint Paul sometimes withstood Saint Peter to the face, but their union was in the Heart of Jesus. It is the same with us today. There are many divisions amongst Christian people, but when we are troubled about the divisions in the Church, we can remember that there is one Heart which is always faithful, and if we are tempted to despair of union amongst ourselves, we may, nonetheless, have hope of union in Him.

Our sermons are mostly the way we have of escaping from the hard work of prayer, and apologizing for our sad deficiencies; if we really were holy people, it would be as unnecessary for us to preach as it is for a flower to advertise.

Our Lord gives Himself wholly to each one of us. That is what we almost never do to one another. We give our sympathy perhaps, when someone comes to us in trouble, and that is a great thing to give, but we do not give ourselves. And so, though we help people, we do not really change them. It was because our Lord gave Himself wholly for and to each soul that He changed Mary Magdalene from a sinful woman to a saint, Peter from a weak man to a rock, and Thomas from a doubter to a pillar of the Church.

People's characters are tested in three ways: by the circumstances in which they live, by the people whom they meet, and by the experience of their own failures. Their characters are tested by the degree in which these things draw forth from them love and not bitterness, a humble penitence and dependence upon God and not despair.

We live in an age of challenge. Paganism in splendid apparel offers us a cup of pleasure. If we are to drink it to the full we must die to our Christianity. Christ offers us His cup, and if we are to draw from it the hidden sweetness therein we must die to the paganism of self-interest. The question for the modern man and woman is, "Which sets forth the life more abundant, the propositions of the pagan or the creed of the Christian?" The answer to that question is the deep disillusionment and disappointment and underlying sadness in the lives of men and women of pleasure, and the radiance that shines forth from the divine revelation and is reflected in the lives of the saints and all who have followed in their steps. The best part of our cure is accomplished when we see the beauty and desire to possess it, when we have the will to be made whole.

We are apt to treat sin lightly, and yet, just as an acorn has in it all the potentiality of an oak, and that little thing, left to develop, becomes that immense thing, a great spreading oak, so a little selfishness has in it the potentiality of the crucifixion of Christ. Leave a selfish sin to develop, and there is no human providence which can tell to what that selfishness may develop.

"I could do such a lot," people sometimes say, "if I had the time," or the money, or the ability. That little word "if" makes a tremendous challenge. We are either accidents or animals or the children of God. If we are accidents, there is not much point in life, and we can only wait till that other accident which we call death comes to end this accident which we call existence. If we are animals, we can only live as animals and die as animals and fight as animals. But if we really are the children of God, we must be rising ever to the splendor and royalty of the everlasting Divine Life, to the majesty, glory, and beauty worthy of God. We are called to love Him with all our heart and soul and strength, and our brothers and sisters, our neighbors, as ourselves. It may be that the way of faith will take us through darkness and pain, but if we are the children of God we cannot come down from the cross that proves our faith and our love.

Those brave people who break the ice and bathe in the Serpentine, or climb high mountains, might think contemptuously of some servant of God who practiced great mortifications. But the ascetic after all is only a spiritual athlete, seeking the true dominance over his body. There must be in one way or another the deliberate loss of the material life that the spiritual life may be found. The urge to self-discipline is perhaps the negative part of the adventure, as obedience to the interior call of God is the positive advance to the spiritual goal of the heaven of God's presence, which must be for all eternity the lure of souls.

We can in our own little lives be utterly certain that God always has an alternative, in which the one purpose for which we are here may be fulfilled, if other ways fail. We are on this earth to reveal in human nature the holiness of the children of God. That holiness might be revealed through a successful beneficent business, through the fulfillment of plans well thought out and carried to a right completion, through lives that were healthy and prosperous and surrounded by companies of faithful friends, and through a steady development of goodness in our own souls. But all these things may fail. We may fall away; our fortunes may collapse; our friends may betray us, and we may betray them. There is always God's alternative of a re-

turn through penitence, of a salvation through suffering, of a redemption through pain—always that His
original purpose may be fulfilled. If our lives are wholly
given, we can be sure that they will be guided; if they
are wholly surrendered, we can know that they will be
led back into the way of union with the will of God,
which will be to us peace and to Him glory.

We are all being led, whether we like to admit it or
not, and we are all in some way leading others, because
we cannot help influencing people by the way in which
we live ourselves. We ought to think seriously by what
spirit we are led.

We were created for no other end than this, that we
should worship God to all eternity.

The Holy Spirit is pledged to help us to see things
from the point of view of Jesus. When in our life some
bitter cup comes to us, we shall be able to see in that
cup love's opportunity. If we yield ourselves in prayer
to the Holy Spirit, things will begin to look quite different. As we see things from the supernatural point
of view, we shall begin to meet them by supernatural
methods. That is what conversion means.

Remember that this is true: every life is a witness to
something: there is not a single person who is not
witnessing.

We too live and serve and suffer that the world may
know that we love the Father.

Our Lord Jesus Christ came to change and purify our
thoughts. Many papers suggest that life consists in what

we have, that the true riches are material goods. We learn from our Lord another set of values. He taught the blessedness of poverty as an escape from the bondage of material life, and that life does not consist in what we have but in what we are. We brought nothing into the world, and we can take nothing out of the world. In ourselves is the true happiness or unhappiness, the true riches or poverty.

Interruptions come into every life, and lives are very largely proved by the way in which interruptions are met. If we look back over the course of our lives, most of us will thank God for many of the interruptions, which perhaps revealed to us that some course of action was not right or prevented us from embarking on something that was wrong, or woke us up from soulless complacency. We may be sure that interruptions which are not our own fault have over them the providence of God, and come to us accompanied with the grace of God to draw from them what is for the shaping of our own souls. Interruptions are part of life's vocation, and if we see them in that light, they may alter our arrangements, but they will not alter our direction.

The end of devotion is not to become extraordinarily devout. It is possible to fill one's life with practices of piety, and yet not to get more Christlike. It is possible to spend much time in devotion, and yet to be hard and critical and to lack a missionary and loving spirit. It is a terrible, as well as a salutary, thing to remember that it was devout people at a time of special devotion who killed our Lord.

What are we here for? We are here for exactly the same reason that our Lord was in this world. He has revealed in His life what human life is for. It is for the fulfillment of a perfect sonship. Our Lord has revealed to us the Father; we are in our measure to reveal the Christ. Our Lord bore the world's burden revealing His Father as the everlasting Love. We are, in bearing one another's burdens, revealing the everlasting brotherhood in Christ.

This is one of our Lord's great classic utterances, which are at the very root of His message to men. He said, "The kingdom of God *is*"—not *will be* or *may be*— "within you." There is in every one of us a principle of victorious goodness which is the true kingdom, and that principle is meant to prevail and to become manifest in our lives. People said of Mary of Magdala that she had seven devils. They may have said that the kingdom of the devil was within her, and it was pretty obvious that the kingdom of the devil *was*, as we have often found that the kingdom of the devil is within us. We can see it in others. We say, "Oh, he is past praying for," or, "Oh, you will never do anything with a woman like that." The kingdom of the devil and the kingdom of God are both within us, but the devil is a usurper. The kingdom of God is in every soul, just because this is God's world. That was one of our Lord's great credal affirmations. It is within me, it is within everybody.

We can only have power if we are obedient. If we are disobedient, all power falls from us, because we are living in our own strength, in our own way.

God calls us to *be* much more than to *do*, and what we are becoming matters most to him.

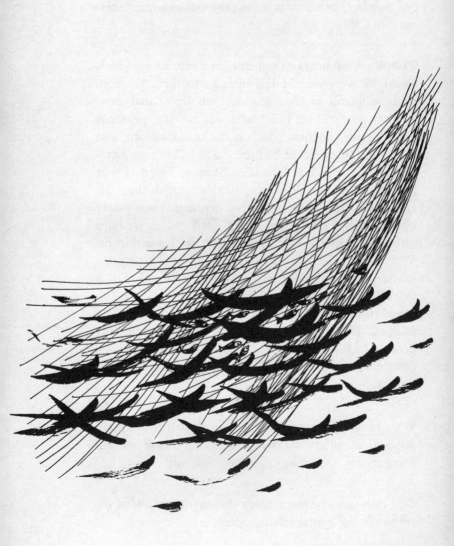

What is my deep desire but just this, that God's will shall be done in me?

It is one thing to know about God: it is another thing to know Him. It is one thing to go to religious occasions; it is another thing to go to God Himself.

It is not much use pointing others to a road along which we ourselves do not propose to go. We can show people the way best by going along it. We can tell of its difficulties only by the honesty of our own experience. We are to be pilgrims, not signposts.

Life was meant to be a walk, a talk, a work with God.

There is an Adamhood to which we are to die: there is a Christhood into which we are to rise.

As soon as we cease to desire, we cease to be truly alive. Life is meant to be a desiring thing. We are meant to be passionate, but the passion of our souls is to flow in God's channels, not the devil's. There is nothing so thrilling as the quest of holiness, there is nothing so dull as sin.

When our Lord said to Saint Peter, "Launch out into the deep, and let down your nets," and the apostle answered, "At Thy word I will," he was not going to do something different to what he had been doing daily, but this very commonplace thing he had been constantly doing he did now with a sense of vocation and as an act of responsive obedience. The sense of vocation may alter the whole condition of a life. It may take a man from an office to the priesthood, as it took Matthew from his customs to his discipleship. It may take a priest into the religious life or out to the mission field. But it may, on the other hand, only change the motive and quality of the life, leaving it the same, but transfigured and vastly enriched, as it is lifted from a profession to a vocation.

As we read the words and meditate on the life of our Lord Jesus Christ, we feel that He is the incarnation of all the spiritual values of life. "There standeth One among you, Whom ye know not." Learning to know that One is the whole of our religion. The knowledge of Him is our heaven.

Life is made up of a continual succession of weanings. "My soul," says the Hebrew poet, "is as a weaned child." When we were babies and our mother laid us down, we cried because we missed the security of our mother's arms. Perhaps when we went to school we were afraid, because it meant leaving the security of home. All our life we fear insecurity. It is the sense of insecurity which looks out from the haunted eyes of the woman making her living on the street, from the eyes of the man who is unemployed. The disillusioned woman, the unemployed man, the bereaved heart, every one from whose world the bottom has fallen out, can hear the echo of their own perplexity, their own anguish, in this cry, "My God, My God, why hast Thou forsaken Me?" What is the answer? When our mother laid us down, when she weaned us, it was the only way in which we could pass to a richer development of our being. We had to pass from a felt security through a felt insecurity to a greater development. A great doctor, Dr. Crichton Miller, said, "People talk about the problem of pain, but for my part I cannot see how in a painless world there could be either intellectual development or moral values." It is facing that insecurity that draws out the manhood of a soul. Our souls are given faculties of thought, conception, imagination. It is the sense of insecurity that draws them out. No more can be asked of love than this, to love on in lovelessness. No more can be asked of faith than this, to trust on in the void. No more can be asked of hope than this, to be heroic and loyal to the last breath, to hope in the character of God. The last great weaning is death. We have to know what it is to pass from the sense of the security of physical experience out into the unseen and unknown. The last Word of all is the final answer, "Into Thy hands I commend My Spirit." All life is a continual process of weaning from something that is good but not yet the best, that we may pass through the sense of insecurity which develops our faculties to the perfect security at last of the presence of God.

We cannot be in a wrong relationship with others if our wills are in union with the will of God.

Some men are very fond of the game of darts. They are always taking aim, and, when they miss, considering why they miss, and learning from their faults and taking aim again. "I must aim a bit higher" or "a bit harder" or "not so hard." So we want to be taking aim and renewing our aim. We must ask ourselves, "Is my life aimless? Is my aim wrong? What should my aim be?" Our aim should be the worship of God and the love of our neighbor. In our self-examination we must consider how much and where and why we fell short of the mark; in our prayer and worship we must renew our aim.

Life finds us out, and our first discovery may be very like the discovery of Saint Peter when he went out and wept bitterly after denying his Lord. But that was not the last word about Simon Peter, nor need our failures ever be the last word about ourselves. We can learn by our mistakes and, if life finds us out, we can find out our God in our life, and through its challenge and His grace bring forth the fruit that shall make us known as His children.

It is an extraordinary thing, but only recently, reading the parable of the Good Samaritan, did I realize how our Lord spoke to the lawyer. The lawyer said, "Who is my neighbor?" and our Lord said, "That is not the point. The point is, to whom are you to be a neighbor?" When He told the story of the Good Samaritan, He did not say who the Samaritan's neighbor was. Certainly the Samaritan would not have thought of a Jew as his neighbor. The question is, "To whom are you to be a neighbor?" It sometimes helps to put things the other way round. People say, "I am not getting much out of the Church." That is not the point. The point is, "What are you putting into the Church?"

Never until our Lord became incarnate did God see in human nature exactly what He wanted to see. We in ourselves are something other than God meant us to be, but our Lord is exactly that which God meant Him to be. In Him we see this human nature of ours, free from all alliance with the smallest imperfection, completely expressing the divine idea which had called it into being.

We are souls athirst for the living God. That is the interpretation of all our restlessness, all our sorrow, all our pain. As our eyes are opened to see Him, our wills are strengthened to choose Him, our souls are inspired to know Him, not only do we cry out for the living God, but in Him we find our rest.

To find the Real we ourselves must be real. We cannot bring God our sins that we may keep them, but we can bring God our temptations that we may overcome them. We may be conscious of great disorder within ourselves and feel that we are full of evil desires, but nonetheless, we can at least desire that our desires may be pure. The wish to will as God wills is itself a prayer spark that He can kindle to a flame, and from such humble but quite honest beginnings souls have often found their way of escape from the mists to the mountains.

We read of stars that are millions of times bigger than our earth, so that our world is smaller than a grain of sand compared with the immensity of the universe and we ourselves less than the tiniest insect. But all of this is as nothing compared with the majesty of the still small voice in the soul of man. When the voice challenges us with the question, "What doest thou here?" we know that, at whatever cost or sacrifice, we can only find peace when we are able to say, "I am here to do Thy will."

A man should ask himself how he can best serve God and his neighbor. When once he has got an answer to that question, he should follow his soul's vision through all things to the end.

Our life is a great adventure, a romance, a splendid and wonderful thing, a quest which was started by God Himself. Our Lord died to redeem our journeying from the only failure which is real failure, and that is spiritual failure. It matters not what may come to us, what may oppose us, what pain or darkness we may go through. The Holy Spirit will teach us in all these things to form the faculties which will fit us to behold the vision of God as through the purging of experience we are re-created according to the likeness of that image wherein the creative mind of God first conceived us.

If a person has a moderate ear for music, he can detect if a piano is very much out of tune; but if it is moderately out of tune, it will not distress him, because his ear is not sufficiently sensitive to detect the discord.

If a soul is spiritually undeveloped, such a soul will feel unhappy if she falls into some great act of selfishness, but otherwise will not be troubled. As a soul attains to a spiritual sensitiveness, so she becomes aware of any taint of self-centeredness and self-will that mars the freedom of her service; she knows when she is out of tune.

We cannot go beyond our light or run ahead of our spiritual experience, but we must be loyal to the light we are able to see. The more we respond to the vision and the pressure of the will of God, the more sensitive will our souls become; and also the judgment on neglect and disobedience will always be a deadening of our sense of sin and appreciation of holiness.

Some people are helped by having a rule, but I think most serious people, though they may never write down a rule or consider that they keep one, do really live by rule. They rise about the same time and retire about the same time; their Bible-reading, prayer time, church attendance, varies very little; they do practically keep a rule. What I feel about a rule myself is that one wants to be very clear that it is a *rule*, *something below which one will not let oneself drop*; it is not an *ideal,* something to which one is trying to soar. A rule is a bad thing if one is content with it. Contentment is the death of art and all achievement. There never was a contented artist or a contented saint. "A Christian who is a contented Christian is not a Christian," said Luther once. All beauty, spiritual and artistic, is ever beckoning the disciple to come up higher. "Be ye perfect," said our Lord, and that gives us the blessed discontentment with ourselves and the exhilaration of the quest for the Divine Beauty.

As a matter of fact all education is on much the same lines: (1) you find someone who can paint; (2) you watch that person painting; (3) you go away and try to paint yourself; (4) you bring back what you have done to the Master for criticism and correction; (5) you try again.

So a student learns to paint. Substitute for "student" the word "disciple"; and for "someone who can paint" "the Incarnate Christ," and for "learning to paint" all that we mean by religion—learning to live, to love, to suffer, to succeed, to fail, to worship, to die—and your spiritual education will follow the lines of all education.

The important thing is, that you should have a quiet time in each day enclosed for God; the time you must fence and keep with absolute strictness; the way you spend it and the technique you bring to bear in it, may be marked by great freedom.

Saint John the Baptist stands out pre-eminent for the complete integrity of his character. He was ready to decrease in order that Christ might increase, to sacrifice himself wholly for the cause. Many people are ready to fight for a good cause, provided they themselves are in the front rank, but when for the good of the cause it would be better for them to give place to another, they go out of the battle altogether. Saint John was completely ready to take a lower place, and to see his own disciples leave him and follow Jesus. Again, he was ready to say the same thing in any company. He preached the same doctrine in the royal chapel as in the market-place, and, if he taught the publicans that they must give up their sins, he also denounced the crime of Herod, who was living with his brother's wife. He gave our Lord that purest devotion, that he was ready to leave Jesus for Jesus' sake, to go from the manifest presence in the home of Nazareth to labor in the wilderness for the coming of the Kingdom.

It is part of the training of our character that we should recognize that there is much we cannot do; all we can do is to make ourselves instruments in God's hands, to use or lay aside. Our part may be to sow that others may reap, and we must be ready to stand aside for the good of the cause. We must try to get that integrity of character which will make us perfect servants in the cause of the kingdom. There is often a vocation to follow Saint John the Baptist in leaving conditions where we have spiritual luxury, to labor in self-effacing ways that in some wilderness the Faith may be born.

Poems

A SOUL'S NIGHT

Sweet Lord, the night grows dark and I
Am filled with nameless fears,
My mind just moans, my eyes are dry,
Too weary even for tears;
And my soul is haunted by my sins
And the ghosts of other years.

Must I lie staring at the dark
Till the day dawns bald and grey?
No silver star, no morning lark,
Only another day!
Sweet Lord, have mercy on a soul
Too sore, too scared to pray.

I saw a picture once in France,
How it comes back to me,
That wan, sad Christ of Carrière
In a mist of agony,
With the blessed Mother standing there
Sharing His Calvary.

I will not ask escape from pain,
Nor crave unclouded skies;
If pain may mirror back Thy pain
And search such mysteries—
But I know that I shall sleep again,
For Love hath kissed my eyes!

SILENCES

How many silences there are—
 The winter's white tranquillity;
The silver silence of a star;
 The moon's pure queenly sovereignty;

The awful silences of hate;
 Still water's deep profundity;
The silent swiftness of the spate;
 And all sly, crouching cruelty;

The silence of the dawning day;
 The velvet silence of the night;
Their silence who have learned to pray;
 The silence of the Infinite;

The sweet green silence of the glade;
 Blue silences of twilight dear;
Their silence who are not afraid
 And wait for Truth their cause to clear;

The silence of the Stable Cave,
 When all His visitors had gone
And He slept sound Who came to save,
 And Mary pondered there alone;

The silence when He bowed His head
 After the loud last bitter cry,
When Mary knew her Babe was dead
 And the sun set on Calvary;

The silence of the Garden shrine
    Beneath the star-strewn Syrian sky,
Where lay the Lord of life divine,
    Wrapped in death's silent mystery.

How many silences there are,
    In earth below, in heaven above,
And best and sweetest of them far,
    The golden silences of love.

THE BIRCH COPSE

When I can go just where I want to go,
There is a copse of birch-trees that I know;
And, as in Eden Adam walked with God,
When in that quiet aisle my feet have trod
I have found peace among the silver trees,
Known comfort in the cool kiss of the breeze
Heard music in its whisper, and have known
Most certainly that I was not alone!

THE WAY HOME

The sunset lights the traveller's face
　　As he tramps along with zest;
He breasts the hill with quickened pace
　　For his home is in the west;
　　　　And whatever roads a man may roam,
　　　　The best of all is the one way home!

'Tis steep and dark, the sun goes down,
　　Life's journey is well nigh done—
Heed not the thorns, they shall make a crown
　　In the City that needs no sun!
　　　　For whatever roads a man may roam,
　　　　The will of God is the one way home.

JUNE THOUGHTS

The gleaming river glides between
Broad meadows glad with gold and green;
Radiant with light and rapturous with song
June's shining hours pass along;
And, plucking flowers, moves her following throng.

A thrush sits singing on a willow bough,
Which bends to meet the murmurous water's flow
That makes a soft accompaniment while he sings,
And every trembling leaf with his glad rapture rings.

Ah, is Time's pageant, passing day by day,
This change from grey to green, from gold to grey,
This sighing, singing circle of the year,
A rather long procession ending here
And never really leading anywhere?

Ah, no! Life's river seeks the sea of God;
Life's sin may find the cleansing of His blood.
Not only wisdom made the world so fair,
But Love, Who, sparing others, did not spare
Himself the cruel Cross, if He might lead
To living waters and green pastures there.

THE SACRED WOUNDS

O dearest Lord, Thy sacred Brow
  With thorns was pierced for me:
O pour Thy blessing on my head,
  That I may think for Thee.

O dearest Lord, Thy sacred Hands
  With nails were pierced for me;
O send Thy blessing on my hands,
  That they may work for Thee.

O dearest Lord, Thy sacred Feet
  With nails were pierced for me;
O send Thy blessing on my feet,
  That they may follow Thee.

O dearest Lord, Thy sacred Heart
  With spear was pierced for me:
O shed Thy blessing on my heart,
  That I may live for Thee.

A PRAYER

Show me Thy light when the dawn is dim,
And Heaven still holds the morning star,
When the gates of the East are just ajar,
To gild with gold the earth's round rim.

> After the night,
> Dear Lord, I pray,
> Through this new day
> Give me Thy light.

Give me Thy grace, for the way is clear,
And the road is lone and steep and long.
O succour me and make me strong,
Thy light hath shown me all I fear.

> Through the long day,
> Till fall of night,
> Grant me Thy grace
> To bear Thy light.

Give me Thy love, for love alone
Shall find the rose upon the thorn,
And in that last unending morn
Shall see Thy face, O Holy One.

> For love is grace,
> And love is light,
> And love the morn
> That ends the night.

THE CHRIST OF UNCERTAIN DAYS

Lord, we are living in uncertain days,
    And who can tell what any hour will bring?
The peradventure of our wandering ways
    Is known to Thee, and Thou art still the King
Omnipotent, Who reigneth over all,
Grant us in quietness to hear Thy call.

For Thou art surely calling, calling still
    To "come up higher" in the quest of Love,
To drink the Father's cup and do His will
    And in our life's adventure here to prove
That we can seek—not peace at any price—
But at all costs to make Love's sacrifice.

And Thou, Who callest, hast Thyself alone
    Trodden the wine-press of Thy Calvary.
The sin of man has given Thee a stone,
    Thou gavest back the Bread of Charity;
And in the power of that Bread may we
Win, in the day of hate, Love's victory!

LOVE'S ARGUMENT

I took Love to task;
"Behold," I said,
"How many a weary one
Hath only straw to lie upon."
"There will I lay my head,"
Said Love, "'tis straw I ask."

I took Love to task;
"Behold," I said,
"How many thorns there be
To rend and pierce with treachery
Our lives." Love bent Him down
And took the thorns and made of them
A crown!

I took Love to task;
"Behold," I said,
"Yon gibbet with its burden dread.
Hate reigns!" Love answered me,
"I found a throne like that
On Calvary."

I said to Love,
"Thy law is much too hard,
I cannot follow Thee,"
Love stretched forth mighty arms
And said, "Come, child,
I'll carry thee!"

CHILL DAYS

Outside the rain and the drear drab street,
And the dark-coated silent men,
And the patter and tramp of the worker's feet
As it flows to the city and ebbs again
In the evening, this tide of women and men.

And here I kneel at Thine Altar, Lord,
And one or two who are trying to pray
That Thy Kingdom may come and Thy Sovereign
        Word
May prevail, and that men may see that day
When, as the waters that cover the sea,
Thy glory shall flood the world to be!

Thy Kingdom come! Thy Kingdom come!
Sometimes how far away it seems,
A pretty piece of poetry
Fashioned of stuff of children's dreams.
'Tis we make fanciful the fact
Remake the Manger, gem the Cross,
Thine is the dread deliberate act
That faced the fear and risked the loss.
Life only finds reality
At Bethlehem and Calvary.

"WHY?"

"My God, My Father, why?"
That was Thy piteous cry,
Sweet Lord, on Calvary.

In all perplexity,
Echoing agelessly,
Cometh that cry to me;

When I must stand and see
Some one apparently
Suffering uselessly;

Or worse than any pain
Look on a life insane
Where death would seem a gain;

'Tis then Thy questioning cry,
"My God, My Father, why?"
Comforteth me greatly.

If Thou could'st question so,
I can through darkness go,
Contented not to know.

Yea, I can also see
How life's dark night may be
Love's opportunity.

Lord, I was made for Thee,
So let me rest
Not otherwise than on Thy breast.
Let the pure thought of Thee
Quiet my mind,
In Thy dear Heart my heart
Its haven find.
Yet, let myself, this little soul,
Come to so great a goal.
For though of clay Thou madest me,
My clay was touched with Thine eternity,
And I am "restless till I rest in Thee."

CONTRAST

I saw the morn break glorious o'er the sea
With all the ritual of its pageantry:
Soft herald lights shone first, then splendidly
Crimson and gold gave welcome royally:
The dim dawn curtains parted, and the sun,
A great gold circle, slowly, solemnly,
Proclaiming that a new day had begun,
Rose from his palace underneath the sea.

From that magnificence I went my way
Down to the village church below the hill,
And there with simple souls I knelt to pray,
With them to learn submission to His will
Who with true poverty could be content;
And, as my Lord in mercy came to me
In the small circle of the Sacrament,
I marvelled at His deep humility.

O TARRY THOU THE LORD'S LEISURE

What will the day bring forth? Dim glows the morn,
One lone star glitters in the chill wan sky,
And ere the evening's radiance one is born,
And weeping eyes have watched another die.
What will the day bring forth?

The fruit was ripest when to earth it fell,
The cup was spilt ere laughing lips could taste,
The one most trusted could his Master sell,
Is all our painful striving weary waste?
What will the day bring forth?

Take heart, for Love still triumphs over all,
"Much fruit" can bless the dying of the corn,
He rose the highest Who feared not to fall,
He reigns forever Who was crowned with Thorn.
Let come what will,
Love triumphs over all.

THE DIVINE FAREWELL

It is a human thing to say farewell,
Our life is ever haunted with "good-byes":
Yea, as we look into our best friend's eyes,
This is the surest thing that we can tell—
There comes a day when we must say farewell.

And He Who died for us on Calvary
Shared this with us, as Holy Scripture tells:
The saddest, sweetest, fondest of farewells
Christ to His Mother spake, when from the tree
He gave her to Saint John and you and me.

And hope was child of that pure travail pain:
The sure and certain hope to meet again.

COMMUNION IN A COUNTRY CHURCH

I brushed the dew-drenched daisies on the lawn,
I passed the silent cattle in the field
And laborers going out to work at dawn
To seek such store as the good earth should yield.
One silver star was set in the pale gold
Like a dropped jewel of the passing night.
A white mist hung over some sleeping fold
Like a gauze curtain in the morning light:
So—past the river and the little street,
The grey old tombs and solemn ancient yews,
Into the Holy Place, Thy Mercy Seat,
Where Thou, the Lord of all, didst not refuse
To give to me a sinner that same morn,
To hold and keep the Secret of the Dawn.

GROWING OLD

I don't want to be a coward,
But I want to see my way,
I dread the twilight deepening to night;
And when I kneel before Thee I've so little now to
    say,
But Lord, I want my silence to be right.

I hate to hurt another,
But often now I find
My thoughts go wandering so far away,
That I may neglect my neighbor, who thinks that
    I'm unkind;
Lord, help me to keep courteous all the way.

I seem to see the gleaming,
Beyond the purple hills,
Of the radiance of the city of my King;
But I don't want to be dreaming and forgetting
    human ills,
And the doing of the practical next thing.

If I might make petition,
I think that I would pray
To be spared a waiting time of uselessness;
That when past active service Thou would'st call me
    right away;
Yet, Lord, deliver me from wilfulness.

HORIZONS

The hills outlined against the quiet sky
   Enclose the one world visible to me,
But on beyond them through the gloaming fly
   Birds soaring home in utter certainty.

'Tis nothing but the measure of my sight,
   That far horizon—real only to me
As a horizon—etched against the light
   Of the sweet evening's dying radiancy.

Death's dim horizon limits vision here,
   But they who pass it, pass but out of sight,
Leaving our darkness, soaring homewards where
   Other horizons lose themselves in light.

Bibliography

BIBLIOGRAPHY

Books by Father Andrew	Symbol Used in Bibliography
ADVENTURE OF FAITH	AF
ADVENTURE OF PRAYER	AP
CHRIST THE COMPANION	CC
IN THE SILENCE	IS
LIFE AND LETTERS OF FATHER ANDREW	LL
THE LIGHT OF THE WORLD	LW
MEDITATIONS FOR EVERY DAY	Me
POEMS	Po
THE PATTERN PRAYER	PP
PRAYERS FROM FATHER ANDREW	Pr
SELECTIONS FROM THE PSALMS	SP
SEVEN SIGNS OF CHRIST	SS
SEVEN WORDS FROM THE CROSS	SW
THE WAY OF VICTORY	WV

BIBLIOGRAPHY ·

Page	Reference
16.	WV-117; Me-80; SW-32; SW-38, 40
17.	SW-40-41; LL-175
18.	LL-175; SW-46; PP-55; Me-171; Me-164; SW-29
19.	Me-198; CC-110; WV-129
20.	WV-129; IS-170; Me-102; IS-65; LL-118; WV-3
21.	WV-3; SW-57; PP-30; Me-282
22.	Me-282
24.	SW-59; LL-187; SW-41; LL-113; AF-64
25.	AF-64; WV-37; SS-72; WV-38; Me-167; Pr-12; Me-100
26.	Me-100; SW-45; IS-144
27.	IS-144; PP-36
28.	PP-37
30.	Me-53; IS-23
31.	CC-36
32.	CC-30; Me-160; Me-253; SS-52
33.	SS-52; Me-166; SS-50; CC-73
34.	CC-73; Me-240; LL-113
36.	CC-120; Me-18; IS-85
37.	IS-85; CC-90; Me-222
38.	Me-222
40.	Me-91; IS-83; LL-210; AP-25
41.	AP-25; AP-viii; Me-164; AP-1; CC-66
42.	CC-66; WV-168; WV-95
43.	WV-95; AP-v; IS-41; IS-43; AP-32
44.	AP-32; SW-25; Pr-26
46.	WV-90; Me-137
47.	Me-137; Me-305; LL-230
48.	LL-230; Me-357
49.	Me-357; PP-39; SS-61; Me-284
50.	Me-284; CC-101
51.	CC-101; LW-59; SS-21
52.	SS-21
54.	Me-143; SS-32; Me-22; PP-76
55.	PP-76; SP-56
56.	SP-56; PP-51; LW-10; IS-94

BIBLIOGRAPHY ·

Page   *Reference*

 97. LL-218; Me-204
 98. Me-204
101. Po-22
102. Po-120
103. Po-120; Po-138
104. Po-66
105. Po-140
106. Po-50
107. Po-11
108. Po-126
109. Po-3
110. Po-21
111. Pr-18
112. Pr-21
113. Po-106
114. Po-5
115. CC-3
116. Po-5
117. Po-57
118. Po-61